COURAGE

TO CONNECT

Stories that encourage
meaningful connection in your life

MARK OSTACH

1st Edition
ISBN 978-1-7353481-0-0
MyMentalSpace, LLC

Dedication

This book is dedicated to Jobie and Mila.
Your mother and I love you to the moon, stars, and back again.
May you embrace the way God has made you and always
remember to share your heart with the world.

Do You Need More Courage in Your Life?

Courage to Connect is a book full of personal stories & helpful resources that are intended to improve your relationships and create more meaningful connections in your life.

In This Book You Will...

• Discover areas of your life that require restoration

• Learn how to become more empathetic

• Recognize moments to be more vulnerable

• Be encouraged to share your story

• Improve your digital well-being

• Work on your mental & emotional health

• Find new ways to lead with courage

By the end of this book, you'll be well on your way to building more meaningful connections both online and offline, leaving you filled with a newfound courage to connect.

HOW TO READ THIS BOOK

At the end of each story you'll be prompted to connect with courage. Each prompt will have a key action associated with it. Below are brief descriptions and icons representing each call to action you will experience along the way:

 Write – You'll want to have something to write with nearby to help put your thoughts into action.

 Share – Getting personal online and offline can be great ways to share your story and support those around you.

 Connect – Be inspired with meaningful ways to reach out and further connect with others.

contents

Forward

Anyone looking for a fresh look at life will receive it from this book.

Mark's ability to bring comfort, hope, and direction for overcoming the chaos of restlessness in life will help you gain courage in creating more meaningful relationships.

Using wisdom gained from his passion and insights, he takes us into his own journey and connects us to processes toward new freedoms.

Having been given the privilege of knowing Mark for many years as a mentor and friend, I have seen him use his many talents and opportunities to see values and problems clearly and then wholeheartedly work toward solutions.

You will laugh, cry, and be encouraged to make changes to enhance your life.

As good as this book is, you will be better served if you arrange to meet with him in person.

Loren Siffring M.D.

COURAGE

The root of the word **courage** is 'cor' – the Latin word for **heart**. In one of its earliest forms, the word **courage** meant "To speak one's mind by telling all one's heart."

CONNECT

The root of the word **connect** is 'con' – the Latin word for **together**. In one of its earliest forms, the word **connect** meant "To be united together physically."

Introduction

I'm a big fan of Brené Brown's work. Her TED talk has 48 million views and she is a leading researcher in empathy, courage, and vulnerability. These three things all relate to human connection and continue to grow in importance to the livelihood of our homes and workplaces. Furthermore, as our digital life continues to consume more of our time, our emotional skills can become desensitized which can weaken our ability to display empathy, courage, and vulnerability.

Personally, I've been doing work around human connection for the past ten years – from creating software to help you better manage your time online to speaking throughout the country advocating for digital wellness practices within organizations, schools, and churches. My work is personal as I've observed firsthand how smartphones and the content behind them impact our physical, emotional, and spiritual health. Don't get me wrong – I love what technology has allowed us to do. We can connect in an instant to family across the globe and the way to do business has changed the landscape of our economy. All of these things are wonderful, however, with innovation always comes change. One major takeaway that I've gained is that no matter how much technology changes the way we interact, we still need in-person connections or we will fall victim to a lonely life.

As loneliness continues to mount, our society is in need of new and meaningful ways to create connection. I believe that this requires courage. When reading through some of Brené Brown's work on courage, I stumbled across her writing below that influenced the formation of this book and my own definition of courage.

"The root of the word courage is cor – the Latin word for heart. In one of its earliest forms, the word courage had a very different definition than it does today. Courage originally meant "To speak one's mind by telling all one's heart."

Over time, this definition has changed, and today courage is more synonymous with being heroic. Heroics is important and we certainly need heroes, but I think we've lost touch with the idea that speaking honestly and openly about who we are, about what we're feeling, and about our experiences (good and bad) is the definition of courage.

Heroics is often about putting our life on the line. Ordinary courage is about putting our vulnerability on the line. In today's world that's pretty extraordinary."

From this point forward in the book, I ask that you embrace the original definition of the word courage. While we shift our understanding, let's look at another word that's evolving in its meaning. The word "connect" has been going through some major transformation.

In one of its earliest forms, the word connect meant "To be united together physically." As I write these words, our entire world is redefining what it means to connect. In the midst of the COVID-19 pandemic of 2020, our connections have been restricted to Zoom meetings and social distancing. The entire globe has been put on quarantine, and the pace of our life outside of our homes has come to a halt. Overnight, the interactions that shaped human connection have been turned upside down. For example:

- Babies are being born with only one person allowed in the hospital room.

- People are dying with nobody by their side.

- Weddings are happening virtually.

- Funerals are being streamed online.

- Birthday parades are a weekly scheduled event.

- Nursing homes have visitors pressed against the windows.

- Preschool students are learning their alphabets over Zoom.

- College students are graduating at home with virtual commencement speeches.

There is no doubt that the way we connect will forever be changed. A new normal is being birthed from this pandemic. As we become more reliant on our virtual connections, I believe we cannot lose sight of our lives offline:

lives outside of our screens, life where human connection was meant to dwell – in person, sharing eye contact, and embracing physical touch.

These new challenges will require us to explore new ways to connect, new ways to be in community, and new ways to find courage to do so.

This book is broken down into small personal stories and helpful resources on ways to create meaningful connections in your life. At the end of each story, you'll be prompted with questions on how you can 'connect with courage' both online and offline. Sometimes you'll be asked to reflect and write. Other times you'll be encouraged to share something vulnerable online. My hope is that these moments invite you to take action towards a life of sharing your whole heart with those around you. But before we dive into the stories, let me share a little bit about the me.

About Me

Sharing my whole heart comes naturally.

I'm an empath, which means that I'm highly aware of the emotions of those around me. This can be both a blessing and a curse. My enneagram number is a 2 (the helper) which means that I'm good at connecting with people and bringing out the potential in others. To top things off, every time I take the *5 Love Languages* assessment by Gary Chapman, I score high for *physical touch* and *words of affirmation*. All of these personality characteristics have provided me with an open heart and a natural draw towards people. My hunch is all of this started from birth.

I was born in 1981 – the same year that Justin Timberlake and Brittany Spears were born. Although I can't quite dance like them, I have always felt a connection to music. As a child, I had big plans to become famous and began playing the piano and writing songs at an early age. I eventually learned to wear clothes while playing music ;-).

The second child of four, I was raised in a loving home in a neighborhood in southeast Michigan. Our annual holiday picture was taken in a Sears photography studio dressed in sweaters and turtlenecks as we posed with smiles. Oh, the joy of being a child of the 80's!

Our neighborhood was full of kids my age, and there was never a summer that wasn't packed with pool parties and flashlight tag. Each Sunday in the fall consisted of three football games as my siblings and I covered each level of the Pop Warner football teams. We would end the day with dinner around the table discussing the weekend's events. Just about the time Alf would come on TV, we would make sure our Trapper Keepers were packed with pencils and paper as we prepared to tackle the epic challenges of middle school. Those were the days!

As I approach my 39th birthday, I'm a proud husband of eight years and father of two beautiful children. Although the picture at right is Instagram worthy, my experiences as a husband and father have been chalked full of ups and downs with many lessons learned.

I've learned that children invite you into the intersection of chaos and joy. I've learned that conflict can be good with your spouse so long as you lean in towards each other when it's over and not turn away from one another. I've learned that finishing writing a book during a global pandemic with two young children at home is enough to make a grown man cry. I've also learned that no matter how old I am, the more grateful I grow. I'm always seeking a deeper connection to life.

Seeking My Own Connection

You know how people collect things like stamps, coins, or cars? Well, I used to collect domains. Yes, website domains. My collection once totaled 47. The bulk of them were based on ideas in or around digital wellness or ways that we could disconnect from technology in order to reconnect with ourselves and those around us. Here are a few examples along with a brief description on what I planned to use them for:

1. TheFacebookChallenge.com – Getting people to go off FB for 30 days.

2. MyMentalSpace.com – An online browser plug-in I created to self-manage your time online.

3. InternetUseDisorder.Co – The formal name that psychologists refer to as Internet Addiction.

4. DigitalDietGuy.com – An alias I had developed for a few years.

5. RestYourPhone.com – Think of Driver's Education for first-time cell phone users.

6. TechnoBrainBurnOut.com – A site dedicated to resources to prevent stress caused from the web.

7. BlockMyCalls.com – An app to help you take a break from your phone.

8. MyPhoneBelt.com – An app that would "buckle up" (prevent you from making calls) while driving.

9. TheShutDownLaw.com – An actual law in Korea that shuts down the Internet for minors.

10. MyDigitalDiets.com – A digital wellness social movement I was hoping to launch.

11. DigitalDiets.com – Pretty much the same idea as above with a different name.

12. DigitalDietChallenge.com – Ditto x 2.

There are two things you can infer from this list – I'm impulsive and that it's been on my heart for over ten years to advocate for a more connected life. Since meeting my wife, my domain count has dropped to 13. I'll soon be at single digits.

In all seriousness, what was I thinking? Why did I go on a domain-buying rampage? Looking back, I think I know the answer.

I wanted people to understand how our life online impacts our emotions and moods. I wanted people to see how the content behind our screens is shaping our sense of worth and purpose. I wanted people to know that our devices can be great tools yet also have the tendency to jeopardize our time for reflection and introspection.

I still want these things. I just don't want all those domains.

So, welcome to my book. This was a feat to write as I've struggled with following through on my ideas for a while (see aforementioned list).

But seriously, welcome.

May you enjoy the stories and resources within these pages, and may they provide the courage for you to share your whole heart.

"Storytelling is the most powerful way to put ideas into the world today."

— ROBERT MCKEE

STORIES

The following stories are personal experiences that have reminded me to embrace the need for human connection. These stories are intended to make you laugh, smile, cry, and reflect on the relationships that exist in your life across family, friends, work, and community.

"Always trust your gut, it knows what your head hasn't figured out yet."

— UNKNOWN

BEHIND THE
SCENES

I recently had the privilege of sitting down with Alicia Smith from Channel 7 to discuss "5 Ways to Improve Our Digital Well Being." The interview went great, and I was thankful for the opportunity to have my work on digital wellness shared with a wider audience. However, as the interview was wrapping, up a more significant story unfolded.

5 WAYS TO IMPROVE YOUR DIGITAL WELL-BEING

Behind the Scenes

A few months before the interview, I was leaving lunch from one of my regular spots on a Friday afternoon. As I walked down Woodward Avenue in the heart of downtown Detroit, my eyes became locked on a homeless man who was sitting on the sidewalk. I often stop and say hi to those I walk by, yet this time was different. I felt a profound draw to him. I sat down next to him and spent a few moments exchanging pleasantries. These few moments turned into a few hours and a connection that I will never forget.

Purposely Connected

This new friend, who I'll call Devon, had a heavy sadness in his eyes. His body was rigid with shame and his voice trembled when he spoke. His eyes filled with tears as our conversation began to move past the surface. I learned that he had been on his own since he was 14 years old (he's now in his late 20's). He had been sleeping on the streets for the past month after being released from a six-month stint in jail. The more I learned, the more my heart sprouted with hope for him. I saw past his sadness and into his spirit. I could see his potential for greatness and his need for help. I also discovered that he was recently offered a job at a local restaurant washing dishes. His job offer came directly after he was digging through a dumpster in search of some food. The restaurant manager said that if he could maintain proper hygiene, he'd hire him on the spot.

Deeper Than My Pockets

I wanted to give Devon some money and wish him well. I wanted to go back to the office, send a few emails, then head home to my family for the weekend. I wanted to wave a magic wand and fix all of his pain. However, I knew the best thing I could do was help him find a shower. After a quick stop at a corner store for some basic hygiene products, a few snacks, and a new shirt, we began our search for a hotel.

As we walked, I learned more about his story. He never met his biological mom (yet her name was tattooed across his forehead). He was shot last year and died on the operating table before being brought back to life. He was afraid of the pitfalls of his past, yet was determined to crawl his way out from it.

After visiting a handful of hotels, we finally found one that wasn't sold out. As I stood in an extremely long line, I felt my mind begin to make excuses on why I should leave.

What happens if he trashes the room?

How much will this cost?

Will I miss dinner at home with my family?

I decided to do what I always do in times of worry.

I called my wife. She picked up the phone, and I explained to her what was going on. We talked things over, prayed together, and she encouraged me to follow through with securing him a room. And that's what I did.

We rode the elevator up to the fourth floor, and I walked him into his room. After setting the grocery bags of goodies down on his nightstand, I handed him a roll of quarters so he could use the hotel laundry room. He smiled as tears rolled down his cheeks, and I knew this was exactly what he needed.

We locked hands, prayed together, and then made a pact to meet up on Monday in front of the restaurant that was willing to hire him.

Where Did He Go?

Monday came and went. No Devon.

I learned that the restaurant was not able to hire him because he lacked a driver's license. I assumed Devon went back to the streets in search of another job. In the meantime, my wife and I began to think of other ways we could help him. She made a trip to the local camping store to pick him up some gear. She came home with a waterproof backpack, a camping pillow, a water bottle, a rain poncho, a bag full of food, and a handwritten card filled with love and encouragement.

I smiled at her as I knew we were spending energy towards something greater than ourselves.

The new gear was placed in the back of my Jeep, and I was eager to find Devon to give him the items. I began looking for him during my lunch hour and after work. As I walked through the city, I prayed to God to direct me back to Devon like he did that Friday afternoon.

Days went by.

Weeks went by.

No sign of Devon.

I grew discouraged, wondering If I would ever see him again.

Back to the Interview

Toward the end of the shoot with Channel 7, Alicia Smith suggested we get some B-roll footage. She asked me to walk down the street, then turn around and walk back toward the camera. As soon as I took my first step back towards the camera, I noticed a familiar figure out of the corner of my eye. It was Devon! And he was walking right towards me!

We greeted each other with a big hug as tears swelled up in our eyes. Alicia was kind enough to snap this photo as she and the cameraman watched from afar knowing that an emotional reunion had just taken place.

Reflecting Back

As I reflect back upon the events that took place, I'm filled with wonder and humbled by the higher works that unfolded over the previous few months. It's funny to think how much we try to control the outcomes of our lives.

Personally, there is a constant battle in my mind to control things.

I've tried for years to control the success of my speaking business in hopes to one day gain national media coverage.

I tried to control when I'd see Devon next.

I tried to control his employment status by thinking that all he needed was a shower in order to get back to work.

I try to control the way our two toddlers act at home.

I try to control the way my wife reacts to certain things.

I try to control the majority of my day.

Choose to Care – Not to Control

I'm slowly learning that the bulk of life is out of our control. The more we can focus on how we care for people, the more likely we are to appreciate all of the good that exists around us.

My challenge to you is to take today and think about how you can care more for those around you. Don't focus on the outcome or worry if the person is even going to notice.

Instead, just *care for them.*

BTW...

Devon took three showers that night at the hotel.

He checked out early and didn't 'trash' the room.

I also learned that he landed a job at a construction site.

My wife and I continue to pray for him daily.

COURAGE TO CONNECT OFFLINE

Think of someone today that needs some extra care. It could be someone in your family, an old friend, or even a neighbor. Now think about an act of kindness you could offer this person. It could be a phone call, running an errand for them, or just sending a card in the mail. Whatever comes to mind, take a few minutes and write it down below.

COURAGE TO CONNECT ONLINE

Giving our time, energy, and finances can be a scary thing. However, it can be extremely rewarding when we know that we are offering our resources without expectations of getting anything in return. My challenge to you is to find a person or organization that is in need. There is no shortage of GoFundMe Campaigns for nonprofits that could benefit from your generosity online. Keep in mind, giving doesn't always require money. It could be your time or your desire to understand what people need and where you can help. Make some time this week to research and respond to someone in need.

"Music produces a kind of pleasure which human nature cannot do without."

– CONFUCIUS

A NIGHT
TO REMEMBER

In March of 2019, my father nearly died of congestive heart failure. Thankfully, he made a swift recovery and has a new lease on life. This new perspective has brought back an aspect of our friendship that had been missing for the last five years. This was best expressed in the summer of 2019 when we attended a concert featuring Kenny G at The Aretha Franklin Amphitheater in Detroit.

Why Kenny G?

Of all the artists performing at The Aretha that summer (including Snoop Dogg), I picked Kenny G – the best saxophone player alive today! Don't get me wrong, I'm not a mega fan, but his music represents a sacred season in my life – a time from the late 80's and early 90's when I was but a young man, before I felt the responsibilities and pressure of adult life.

I've learned that music has the ability to cut through the scars of our past and re-create those sacred moments of our yesteryears. For me, I remember being in middle school when our weekends were packed full of sports, family dinners, and going to church on Sundays (often incentivized by a stop at the local donut bar after service).

I specifically recall that my dad would clean the house like a crazy man every Saturday. If I close my eyes, I can still see the sun shining into our house while Kenny G's latest album flooded the lower level of our home as the smell of Windex filled the air. It seems but a distant dream, yet holds a special place in my heart.

A Dream Come True

I've learned that God speaks to me through mental images that come to my mind and then continue to rehearse until the event or situation has manifested. This has taken me a few decades to realize, but with some discernment, I find myself pursuing these promptings with more confidence. This held true for the Kenny G concert as I kept seeing my dad and I at the show together as soon as I heard Kenny was coming into town. But what I didn't imagine was how God was orchestrating a night that would leave my father's spirit turned inside out.

At the time, I was working for a brand strategy studio called Skidmore. I called in a favor from a client and new friend who ran the concert venue we recently rebranded. She assured me we would have good seats and VIP parking where the artists park. When we arrived, we walked into the back office where the green room was and to our surprise bumped into Kenny G himself right before the show started! After an exchange of pleasantries

and a photo, my dad looked at me and said, "Did you plan this?" I looked at him with a smile and said, "Nope." He was on cloud nine!

The Best Seat in the House

We were riding high and ready to enter the venue. We got to the tenth row where our seats were located, yet chose to sit in a pair of aisle seats that were open. They weren't technically ours, but they allowed my dad to stretch his legs out and rest his walking cane.

Before too long, we were asked to move as the actual ticket holders of the seats arrived. We stood up feeling a touch disappointed, but we decided to test our luck one more time and sit a row behind us that kept us in the aisle. I share the details of our game of musical chairs because what proceeded next was nothing short of a divine seating arrangement.

The lights began to dim. The summer breeze swept in off the Detroit River and was moving through the 10,000-person amphitheater while the sun was setting. It was a perfect summer night. As the crowd began to grow in excitement for the opening performance, the bass player from the band snuck off the stage and into the center aisle carrying a square crate. He placed the crate right in the aisle way directly in front of my dad. He then looked at him and said, "You've got the best seat in the house."

Before you knew it, the first note from Kenny G's saxophone filled the entire place. But he wasn't on stage! We couldn't quite tell where he was entering from. Then the crowd erupted as we all turned around to see Kenny G coming down the center aisle from the back of the venue.

He continued to slowly stroll down the steps as he warmed up his lungs. I could feel my dad's heart began to race as Kenny G came closer and closer, eventually landing right in front of my dad!

He stepped up on the crate and began to play his opening set within an arm's reach from my dad and I. We were speechless. We listened to every note pouring out of the saxophone while embracing each other with tears in our eyes and the same sense of freedom that used to exist in the space that filled our family room on Saturday mornings.

The Air in Your Lungs

Life is so damn precious. Yet we find ourselves overworked, over worried, and often filling our days with distractions and vices to cover up the pain that's buried inside each of us. And yet, a simple song, a single note from a saxophone, can transform the spirit and bring about new life in a single breath.

At one-point Kenny G held a single note for over two minutes. It was unbelievable!

What's even more unbelievable is the same air in Kenny G's lungs is the same air that you and I breathe – the same air that keeps us alive during the most trying times of our life. How wonderful is that?

As we slowly walked back to the car, my dad and I reflected on the night and the remarkable experience we shared together. ♪

My hope for you is that you take time to reflect on a remarkable experience that you've shared with someone you love. And if you feel prompted to reach out to someone that's been on your mind, then go do it! You may just end up in the front row creating a night to remember.

COURAGE TO CONNECT OFFLINE

Reconnecting with people in your past can be difficult, especially when there is pain involved.

Take a moment and reflect on someone in your life that you need to reconnect with. As you hold the image of this person in your mind, write a letter to them expressing what you need to let them know. If you don't feel like writing them a letter, give them a call. You may be asking for forgiveness or seeking forgiveness. You may be just reaching out to an old friend whom you've lost touch with. Whatever the case may be, take action and reach out to the person on your mind.

COURAGE TO CONNECT ONLINE

Think back to a song that you really enjoyed from high school. Now find it on YouTube and post it on social media. Tag any of your friends that come to mind and let them know what this song reminds you of. Music has the ability to bring us back together.

"Life is one big road with lots of signs. So when you're riding through the ruts, don't complicate your mind. Flee from hate, mischief, and jealousy. Don't bury your thoughts, put your vision to reality. Wake up and live!"

– BOB MARLEY

I NEEDED
A SIGN

My friend Shawn is extraordinarily creative. His imagination allows him to create just about anything you can think of. One day we built a chalkboard sign to hang on my kids' wooden playhouse.

Proud to Share

I came home from Shawn's excited to show my wife the sign we built and my vision for it. I eagerly took it outside to find the best place to mount it on the playhouse. However, I quickly learned that no matter where I placed the sign, it was going to disrupt the way our kids run around the house. I feared my daughter would hit her face on it as she often was being chased by her older brother. I needed a new plan on how to use the sign.

Plan B

I had another idea on where to mount it. This idea was more for my wife and I than it was for the kids. Let me explain. We have this incredible 60-year-old tree that anchors our backyard. Every morning I go into the yard with our two dogs and walk barefoot over to this giant tree and greet it with a morning stretch. I often wonder what this wise old tree is saying back to me. As I thought about the idea of a talking tree, I realized that this tree would be a great place to mount the sign, especially since we look directly at it when standing in our kitchen. My thought was to write scripture on it to memorize and inspire us. I explained this idea to my wife, which she loved, but I could tell she was eager to evolve my thinking.

"ONE WORD!" She said out loud.

"One word a week to ignite a fire in our bellies and inspire our day."

I smiled at her and thought, "One word it is." :-)

Our First Word

I still needed to paint the sign and get some long screws to mount it to the tree. My building adventure continued as I ran to the hardware store to finish the job. When I returned, I began to sense that I was spending a little too much time on this project. I hurried up and painted the sign to complete the task at hand. As I walked inside the house, I could see the kids were losing steam for the day, dinner wasn't ready, and the excitement of the sign project was fading fast into the sunset.

My wife and I began to bicker about something petty, and it led to one of those arguments when you can't even recall what you are arguing over. I think we were both just feeling tired and 'hangry'! As we found our way into bed, we said our prayers and drifted off to sleep because I knew tomorrow would bring about an apology and a fresh start. The next morning, I woke up to let the dogs out and walked over to the tree. With an extra pep in my step, I proudly stretched up and saw the sign. And there it was! The first word. CHOICE.

"Choice," I thought? What the heck does this mean? This doesn't feel overly inspiring. Heck, it kinda upsets me! I smiled thinking about our argument and reflected on the first word my wife had chosen to write. I'm pretty sure she was reminding me that I have a 'choice' on how I speak to her :) I spent a lot of time that week reflecting on this simple yet powerful word.

We All Have Choices

Choices on the words we use. Choices on how we spend our time. Choices on whom we choose to pour our energy into. It's amazing how a single word can have such an impact on how we feel and act. It can lift us, inspire us, deflate us, and even change our world. As you begin your day, take some time to reflect on the words you speak and the signs all around you. They are often lessons to be used for guidance and growth. And if you are feeling stuck or down on your luck, then you can always just build one!

P.S.

Here are a few more of the words that have spoken to us. May they speak power into you!

COURAGE TO CONNECT OFFLINE

You don't need to build a sign in order to focus on a single word. Grab a sheet of paper or a sticky note and write down a word that you want to focus on for the week. Now tape this word somewhere that you will see it. It could be in your bathroom mirror, your nightstand in your bedroom, or on your refrigerator.

COURAGE TO CONNECT ONLINE

Take a picture of the word you have written for the week. Now post this picture online and let people know why you chose this word. The more personal you can be, the more people will be able to relate to you, helping create more authentic connections.

"Whatever your problem is, the answer is not in the fridge."

— UNKNOWN

THE BROCCOLI TEST

I have to admit – I'm an emotional eater. With all of the fear racing through our world right now, it has amplified my stress eating. My biggest trigger tends to be right after we get the kids to bed. I go into the kitchen and grab a handful of chocolate chips, dried mangoes, or sugary cereal. When I'm really stressed, I'll eat all three. Thankfully, there is a simple mental trick to help break this unconscious pattern: *the broccoli test*.

The Broccoli Test

The next time you feel like stress eating, I want you to close your eyes and picture a piece of broccoli. Imagine a freshly cooked piece like the one shown.

Now ask yourself the following question: "Am I hungry enough to eat this piece of broccoli?" If the answer is yes, then you are *actually* hungry and your body needs fuel. If the answer is no, then you are most likely emotionally eating. At this point, you are better off getting out of the kitchen, taking a few deep breaths, and then asking yourself:

1.   What do I need to let go of?

2.   What am I thinking and believing right now that is not serving me?

Spending a moment answering these questions can help redirect the thoughts and feelings that are driving your emotional eating. This mental trick also applies to the digital calories we consume.

Digital PTSD

Post Traumatic Scroll Disorder (PTSD) happens when we become emotionally impacted by the digital calories we consume when aimlessly scrolling on our phones. Oftentimes, our digital calories lack nutrition and more closely resemble a sugary spread like the snacks pictured. These digital calories can make us feel 'bloated' with worry.

Between the Coronavirus, world politics, and evening news, there is no shortage of headlines that make us emotionally charged and filled with fear. A recent trend called Doom Scrolling is when people are just waking up and checking the headlines from their phone before even getting out of

bed. These digital calories can be hard to avoid, especially when we have the tendency to check our phones more often when we are stressed. This got me thinking – maybe the broccoli test can apply to our digital life!

Take the Digital Broccoli Test

The next time you go to check your phone, ask yourself, "Do I really need to check it right now?" If the answer is no, chances are you are just emotionally checking, looking to fill the moment up with empty digital calories. This is a great reminder to set your phone down and re-establish your focus. And if all else fails, it never hurts to go eat some broccoli! To take the broccoli test and download the picture, please visit www.markostach.com/broccoli-test.

COURAGE TO CONNECT OFFLINE

Think about a recent headline or story online that has been weighing you down. Now find a friend and let them know how this story is making you feel. I've learned that sharing the worries in your heart from what you've seen online is a great way to reduce the burden you may be feeling in that moment. There's a good chance your friend will have something to share as well.

COURAGE TO CONNECT ONLINE

Reach out to someone you feel could benefit from taking the Digital Broccoli Test. Text them the picure of broccoli and explain to them how it works.

"Don't mix your words with your mood; you can change your mood, but you can't take back your words."

– UNKNOWN

QUARANTINE
CONFESSIONS

"F*cking orange!" These were the words our three-year-old daughter exclaimed at the dinner table recently. My wife and I looked at each other stunned while also holding back laughter. "F*cking orange!," she said again while holding the orange in her hand. This time we directed our attention to her and firmly said, "We don't say that word."

Where Did She Hear That?

This was my first thought. Then I felt a deep pit in my stomach as I realized that her mother and I have both had our fair share of emotional outbursts during this season of global quarantine. Don't get me wrong, we aren't using fruit as weapons during our disagreements, but we may have exchanged a word or two that we later regretted saying. I share this with humility, and I know many of you can relate. It's amazing what stress does to our minds and bodies.

You Are What You Eat?

As I shared previously, The Broccoli Test is a great way for us to think twice about the calories we consume online and in our kitchens. The problem is, during the COVID pandemic, there are so many stories, headlines, and nuggets of content filling our pantries and being swallowed up by our minds. This leads many of us to eat a steady diet of six ounces of fear with two sides of stress for three-plus meals a day. These feelings spike our emotional insulin leaving us cranky, tired, and sometimes cursing in front of loved ones! I'm not blaming my word choice on the media, but I am aware that what I consume online directly impacts my thoughts.

Food for Thought

To the right is the cover of the *USA Today* from January 4th, 2006 (before there was fake news). Forty-one hours after an explosion trapped 13 men in a West

Virginia coal mine, family members and a state official said 12 of the miners had been found *alive*. The papers were quick to distribute this miracle story.

Look at the reaction of the faces in this picture – they are full of cheer, relief and match the headline so perfectly. However, just 12 hours after this article was printed, the exact *opposite headline* unfolded as the truth came out that 12 miners had died and only one survived. The paper had the story wrong.

Does Your Cover Story Match the Truth?

Lately my cover story and the things I share online do not match the true story that I'm feeling. For example, I posted this online yesterday after 'homeschooling' my kids while being in the worst mood I've been in all month.

The stress and mental strain of being home with two toddlers, two parents who are self-employed, and too much time-consuming empty digital calories on social media have impacted my words and the way I'm feeling in ways that I'm not proud of. Fortunately, as my mentor tells me....

Be Slow To Speak and Quick To HALT

The acronym HALT stands for Hurt. Angry. Lonely. And Tired. This is a great tool to determine the words you are going to use before expressing them. It's a reminder that before you react to someone, you should first HALT and ask yourself the following questions: Is this person Hurt? Are they feeling Angry? Are they Lonely? Are they Tired?

If the answer is yes to one or more of these, you may want to step back and take a lap around the house or go hide out in your bedroom for a minute. Keep in mind, you can also apply these questions to yourself before reacting in a way that you'd later regret (i.e. Am I hurt? Am I angry?, etc.). I don't always practice this when I'm upset, but the times I get a flash of HALT across my mind, it tends to slow me down. I find this particularly helpful during this unprecedented season we are in.

Before I Go

We all have a desired cover story we are trying to maintain that most likely doesn't match the new reality we are living in. This is very stressful.

The next time you are feeling overwhelmed with emotion and ready to say something that you may regret, take a deep breath and ask yourself the HALT questions. Become aware of what you are feeling and take a mental or physical lap before you express your emotionally-charged words.

Of course, if this doesn't seem to do the trick, you can always just close your eyes and picture a nice round f*cking orange. :)

COURAGE TO CONNECT OFFLINE

Take a moment to take a screenshot of your heart. In general, have you been feeling hurt? Angry? Lonely? Tired? All of the above? Take a moment and write down how you've been feeling.

COURAGE TO CONNECT ONLINE

Sharing our imperfections can help create more authentic connections. Take a minute and share something online that you are embarrassed to admit. It may look different than your Instagram stories, but I promise you it will create a connection with more people than you think!

"I am the light of the world. Whoever follows me will not walk in darkness, but will have the light of life."

– JOHN 8:12

LET THERE BE LIGHT!

Every time I need to cry, I call my mom.

I'm not sure exactly why, but it works like a charm.

Tears of Joy and Sorrow

My parents often join my family at Christmas service each year. One year in particular, I was sitting between my mom and my wife feeling emotional as the candles were lit and we sang "Joy to the World." While holding my mom's hand, I could feel her healing touch and the bond that exists between a mother and son. In an instant I felt a download of emotions from nearly four decades of Christmas services we've attended together.

My other hand held my wife's hand. I could feel the love that exists between us as we try our best to hold down the fort with two toddlers at home. My hand laid upon hers as I felt the rings on her finger, reminding me of our wedding day and the birth of our children.

The hands of these two women created a connection that words cannot describe. Only through tears could I express how I felt. There was so much to be thankful for in this moment, yet so much emotion in a room full of people just like you and I.

Reflecting in the Light

I turned to my mom as she wiped away tears from her check.

I just got done doing the same to mine.

My tears were those of appreciation for the life that God has provided me with.

Yet as of late, I've let the frustrations of life damper the light that shines within.

I've been insensitive to my wife (a lot).

I've been short-tempered with my children.

And I've been feeling rather downcast.

Maybe it's seasonal depression?

Maybe it's because I'm tired?

Or maybe it's because those closest to me are going through difficult times of divorce, disease, and discouragement.

As an EMPATH (a personality type that over empathizes for others), I have the tendency to take on the weight of the world. Sometimes it fills me up and allows me to give to others and not just focus on myself. Other times, I get overwhelmed with emotions, making it hard to sort through the feelings on my heart.

I was reminded today that it's not on me to fix or heal other people's situations. I can only shine the light that exists within me and hope this brings peace and healing.

Let There Be Light!

These four words hold so much.

They were the first words God spoke into the world.

Light was the first thing each of us experienced when entering into the world.

And light was even present at the exact moment each of us was conceived!

Seeing Life in a New Light

Scientists recently discovered that at the exact moment a sperm penetrates an egg, the egg releases billions of zinc atoms that emit light.

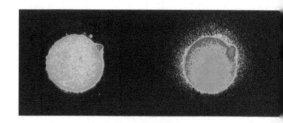

This means that sparks literally fly at the moment of conception! How amazing is this?!? As you sit with this thought, it points to the significance that light has on our existence. It's the source of so many things.

The Source of Vision

Without light, we can't see a thing.

This holds true physically, emotionally, and spiritually.

As we sang together at the end of church, I could literally see hundreds of candles lighting up the room. It was giving light to the darkness in our hearts and allowing us to see the power that comes from a single light that spreads to others.

My Hope for You

Take time to be with the light that shines within you.

Reflect on the things that may be covering it up.

Grab a candle, put on some music, and light up the room that you are in, even if you are by yourself. And know that the greatest source of light is looking for a crack in the door of your heart to shine through!

COURAGE TO CONNECT OFFLINE

Take a deep breath and ask yourself, "What are the things covering my light?" Whatever thoughts come to your mind, begin writing them down here. Don't over-think it, just let your pen flow.

Once you have your list complete, go through each of them individually and ask yourself the following two questions:

1. What am I believing about this item that is not serving me?

2. What do I need to let go of?

COURAGE TO CONNECT ONLINE

Have you noticed how what you view online impacts the way you feel? Sometimes we scroll through social media and find traumatic or disturbing posts that impact our mood. I've noticed that disturbing posts can come from the same people. Take a few minutes on social media and go through your friend lists and determine if there is anyone you need to unfollow.

"A father is neither an anchor to hold us back nor a sail to take us there, but a guiding light whose love shows us the way."

– UNKNOWN

KISS THE KIDS FOR ME

Every time I would talk with my father-in-law, he would always speak the same five words before we finished our time together: *Kiss the kids for me.* As he approached the final days of his life, those words were uttered each time we visited him. My words below are a dedication to the man that I'm proud to have called my Father.

A Father's Love

I've learned so much from Victor Savic. He's modeled the way for me in many ways. A father first, he spent his entire life devoted to providing for his two daughters and wife. He worked tirelessly at various jobs in the food

science and baking industry. Like a loaf of bread rising in the oven, he met each morning with a smile and positive attitude that lifted everyone around him.

Life in The "Old Country"

Born in a small village of the former Yugoslavia, Victor learned first-hand what it meant to live off of the land. He came from nothing. He told me once that his family would sleep in the fields a mile from the village so they could begin harvesting right when they woke up as opposed to wasting time getting ready at home. His first job was to 'watch the cows' when he was ten years old. He once dug a football field worth of land three feet deep in preparation for a vineyard. He dug it in a single summer all by himself.

Odd jobs aside, he used these experiences as building blocks to climb his way out of the life he knew. He was the first person in his entire village to go to college in the United States. I can only imagine the amount of courage it must have taken him to pave this pathway.

A Master Storyteller

We built our friendship out of spending good old-fashioned time together. Before our kids were born, I used to go visit him on Saturday mornings with coffee and bagels. He would slide on his black rubber sandals, grab his cigarettes from the garage, and head out to go sit on the back-porch patio. I would follow behind him after hitting play on the six-disc CD player that was packed with Serbian music. Although I never understood the lyrics, it brought me closer to him and the beautiful culture that he and my mother-in-law came from. The morning sun would shine down as we both enjoyed hot coffee and plain bagels with cream cheese.

I'd listen to his stories for what seemed to be hours on end. It didn't take me long to realize just how smart he was. Wired with a photographic memory and a passion for history, he was able to share life perspectives from just about any corner of the world. His stories would often start with an exact date, "It was June 30th, 1972…" It boggles my mind the way his mind would work. Although his brain was full of facts, his heart was built from solid gold.

Do You Need Anything?

His love came through every time we'd talk. I'd greet him with a big hug and kiss while his thick gray hair and big nose would press against my face. :) He would always look me in the eye and ask me the same set of tender questions:

How are you?

How's Ksenija? (my wife)

How are the kids?

Do you need anything?

All he wanted to do was help. He helped us every time he entered our house, often bringing fresh pita that Nana had cooked and chocolates for the kids. His love was as sincere as the moment he handed over his daughter to me at the altar. His ability to make you feel protected and cared for was proof that the image of God was being reflected from his spirit.

One More Vacation

Days after his pancreatic cancer diagnosis, we were able to book a family vacation at my cousin's cottage. We spent as much time with the family as we could. On one of our last days, a wonderful neighbor offered to take us on a boat ride around the lake. Victor mustered up the energy to walk down the steep steps and the long dock into the pontoon boat. With the summer breeze blowing upon our faces, our smiles shined extra bright as we strolled slowly along the lake soaking in every moment.

Heading Home

After a long month in the hospital, we were able to find a way to bring him home into hospice care for his final days. This was such a blessing as all he

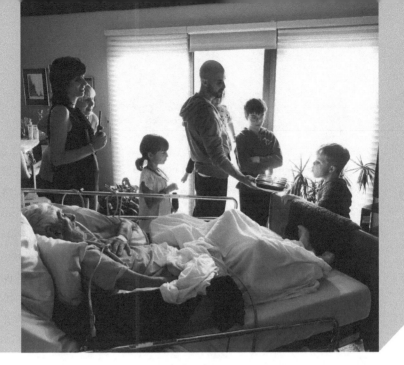

wanted was to be in his family room with the 40-plus years of memories that existed within the walls that surrounded him. Even in his state of illness, he maintained such a positive attitude. His resilience and desire to focus on everyone else was evident. We even had the chance to gather around him and sing happy birthday to our son who was turning five years old. Being at home with his kids and grandkids was the center of his universe.

The Final Night

On the eve before he passed away, we had the chance to gather around his bedside to say our final goodbyes. His eyes were open, his body lay still, and he was unable to speak. His favorite Serbian music played in the background as we wept over him. I held his hand tightly thanking him for all that he had given us when all of a sudden, he lifted his hand up and held my face in the same manner he did with each of the grandchildren. As tears flowed out of my eyes and onto his hand, I knew that he was saying goodbye and reminding me one last time to *Kiss The Kids For Me.*

COURAGE TO CONNECT OFFLINE

Grief can be a challenging emotion to navigate. Oftentimes we associate grief with the death of a loved one. However, grief can happen when we lose other things like a job, a friendship, or a season of our life that is no longer present. Take a few minutes and write down something that you need to grieve. If you are feeling sad, I would encourage you to feel your feelings all the way through. Where is the sadness located in your body? What is the sadness trying to tell you? Our emotions are simply energy in motion (e-motion). They are designed to bring us wisdom. Step into the emotion you are feeling and write down what you need to grieve and what you will miss about it.

COURAGE TO CONNECT ONLINE

Oftentimes emotions like grief and sadness are not things we share online. However, sharing these emotions online invites others to support you and share in your pain. Take a moment to share what you have written. You can choose to post this on social media or just email your words to someone. Writing and releasing are two healthy ways of coping with grief.

"Life doesn't get easier or more forgiving; we get stronger and more resilient."

– STEVE MARABOLI

PRESS ON!

Feeling depressed during the holidays happens to many people. Oftentimes, we enter the end of a year with exhaustion and other negative emotions coursing through our bodies. For me, I often feel sadness, especially when 2019 came to an end. This was the first holiday without my father-in-law. I miss him dearly.

As I write these words, I sip a hot cup of coffee while sitting at a local Panera. With my head down low, I sit with my laptop open as I watch an interview I did with my father-in-law a few months before he passed away. Listening to him in this interview helps prime the emotions that have been trapped in the busyness of the holiday rush.

The lump in my throat has been present for days. My glands feel swollen with repressed tears, yet the distraction of our young children keeps me from fully acknowledging this sadness. Hearing his voice on the video helps me shed a few tears as I keep my head down hoping that nobody will see me.

Beyond the way I'm feeling, my wife is going through her own grieving process while we try to do our best job parenting these energizer bunnies we call our kids. The pressure and pace of our life doesn't always accommodate these seasons of sadness we feel, yet we must press on.

Feeling the Pressure

Everyone feels the pressure. Even the Son of God.

After the Last Supper, Jesus retreated to Mt. Olive and lay face down by an olive tree alone as he cried out to His Father three times to take away the pain, the pain of his eventual crucifixion and the unthinkable pressure of the world's sin soon to be placed upon him. The pressure that Jesus felt was real.

In this era, oil was viewed and used for many spiritual purposes (anointing people, healing the sick, etc.) Moreover, the way the olive oil was made also had a deeper meaning of the pressure that one endures building their faith through life's trials.

The best way to understand this metaphor is to learn how olive oil was pressed. Pictured at right is an ancient olive press. Each time the heavy wooden wheel circled around the olives the weight of the wheel would yield olive oil.

Purpose in the Process

The process of pressing out the oil went through three different presses. Each press grew with weight and intensity similar to each of the three times Jesus cried out. The first press yielded the purest oil that was used for the cooking and consumed by the kings and queens who could afford such a delicacy. The second press squeezed the pulp of the olives and was used to light the lanterns of the middle class who needed the oil to light their homes at night.

Finally, the third press took the last little remnants of the pulp and squeezed out any remaining drops of oil. During this final press there was often dirt, sand, and other elements that weren't intended to be in oil. This oil was used for poor people to cook and eat with. It often was unusable and didn't appear to have much of a purpose at all. However, make no mistake, each press had a purpose. Each press was used for a reason.

We must *press on.*

You Are Not Alone

I understand you have pressure.

You have things going on in your life that you may not post on social media, posts of things that are happening in your world that squeeze your thoughts and your motivation to keep moving forward – everything from

death to divorce, addiction to recovery, sickness to healing, loneliness to loss, and many other olive press moments that you are faced with.

Yet you continue to *press on.*

De-Pressed

The word depression implies that something is pressing down on you, that you are 'de-pressed.' I stumbled upon an image on Facebook and thought it was fitting for this story. As shown below, the word 'depression' when rearranged spells out the phrase *"I pressed on."* How neat is that?

As you reflect on your year, I encourage you to look for all of the areas in your life that you've pressed on. Make a list, tell a friend, or grab a cup of coffee and release the final drops of oil that this year has yielded. Remember, every drop has a purpose for your life.

Keep *pressing on!*

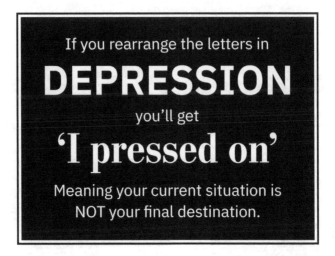

If you rearrange the letters in

DEPRESSION

you'll get

'**I pressed on**'

Meaning your current situation is NOT your final destination.

COURAGE TO CONNECT OFFLINE

Write down something that you feel is weighing you down. It could be the loss of a loved one, a relationship that's on the rocks, or a battle with your health.

Now ask yourself what you think the purpose is in the pressure you are feeling. This may require you to dig deep and remove yourself from the pain of it. Write down what comes to mind below.

COURAGE TO CONNECT ONLINE

Take a moment and reach out to someone you feel has a lot of pressure in their life. Send them an email, a text, or a direct message. Let them know that you are thinking about them and ask them if there is anything they need.

Many plans occupy the mind of a man, but God's purposes will prevail.

– PROVERBS 19:21

FLY LIKE AN EAGLE

Before giving the closing keynote message at the mPARKs Wellness Conference in West Michigan, my eyes were immediately drawn to the center stage upon walking into the ballroom. Directly in front of the podium was a giant painting of an eagle.

As I sat down for the opening remarks, I tapped the person next to me and asked, "What's the story with the eagle painting?" He said to me, "Do you want it? We are about to do a live auction, and it could be yours for the right price." I smiled and [nodded].

Let the Bidding Begin

I've always loved eagles. But what nobody knew, what nobody could know, was that for the last few weeks specifically, I've had an eagle flying alongside me. Not literally of course. But from dreams and meditative visions to conversations with loved ones and strange circumstances, the eagle has been a recurring motif. Seeing this painting, it was clear I was meant to have it. Even before I could finish making the connection between my thoughts and this painting on stage, I surprised myself as my hand went up to place my first bid. A volley of bids went back and forth between me and one other person, who happened to also be named Mark. We were the only two bidding in a room full of 300 people! As the price for the painting began to climb, so did my heart rate. As the volley continued, I thought to myself, "Where in the world would I hang a 4-foot painting of an eagle?" As I processed this thought, my hand began to lower. And just like that, the other Mark placed the winning bid. The eagle had landed. And it wasn't in my court!

Getting Ready for the Main Stage

As my heart rate slowed down, I took a deep breath and began to get my mind ready before my keynote message. As I always do before I go on stage, I write out my intention and a few words that help guide me. This time around, I struggled to focus on my intention at first. My mind was still ruminating on the painting. I couldn't stop thinking that if I would've placed one more bid, I could have won it. I couldn't get this eagle out of my head! As my brain stayed locked on this thought, I heard my wife whisper to me, "Cancel, surrender, release and allow" – a mantra we use to help get our thoughts unstuck. And that's exactly what I did.

It's Go Time!

I entered the stage and was ready to share my message. It was game time. As I walked out and faced the crowd, there it was staring me in the face. The lucky winner had turned the painting toward the stage (away from the audience), and the eagle was facing me! I smiled under my breath as I attempted to push more thoughts of the losing auction behind me.

What Happened Next

As I came off stage, I fielded a few questions from a handful of audience members that stayed back to say hi. As the inquiries faded, my eyes drifted to the side of the ballroom. A group of people stood around the eagle painting. I walked up to them and asked, "What's going on?" A woman spoke up and said "Mark (the winner of the auction) can't fit the painting in his car and gave it to me." I looked at her with my eyes wide opened and asked, "Can I buy it off of you?" She looked back with a smile and said, "You can have it!"

My jaw dropped as my eyes swelled up with tears. Like an eagle with its wings stretched open wide, I held the painting in disbelief of what just happened.

Fly Like an Eagle

It's been shown that eagles can stay perched in the same spot for over 18 hours. As soon as the perfect wind conditions show up, they take off and fly! This allows them to use the least amount of energy when soaring high up in the sky. This sounds like the exact opposite to the amount of thought power and energy I wasted after losing the auction.

Can You Relate?

Do you spend a crazy amount of energy thinking about things that are out of your control? Maybe it's the ruminating thoughts of that career change you've been desiring. Or the cyclical thoughts of self-doubt and fear telling you that you aren't good enough. There are plenty of other things that impact your thought life and ability to soar.

As we wrapped up our time at the conference, people left with new ways to care for themselves, their parks, and the beautiful trails that run through Michigan. In addition to those things, I was left humbled by what had happened. I was reminded that when you give yourself room to 'be still,' it often leads to soaring higher than you could have ever imagined. This requires you to be okay with sitting for a while in whatever situation you are faced with, knowing that perfect wind conditions are soon to come. And when they do, you'll be sure to take off and fly like an eagle!

P.S.

The eagle was painted earlier in the conference by a brilliant keynote speaker named Sam Glenn who paints his pictures without any brushes! His signature is leaving his painting to be auctioned off at the end of each conference. I learned that the highest live auction bid to date for one of his eagle paintings went for $39,000. Unreal.

COURAGE TO CONNECT OFFLINE

What are you currently trying to control? What are your thoughts locked on that's hard for you to let go of? Take a few minutes and write down what comes to mind.

Now take a moment and ask yourself, "What does the opposite of what I'm thinking look like?" This is a great way to see any holes in your thinking and can help reduce the doubts or discouragement that enters your mind.

COURAGE TO CONNECT ONLINE

Cancel. Surrender. Release. Allow.

This is a great way to stop destructive thinking.

First you **cancel** your current thought. Then you **surrender** your desire to control the outcome. Once you've done that, you **release** the worry you are holding onto and **allow** things to unfold as they naturally will. Cancel. Surrender. Release. Allow.

Take a picture and post this online.

If you want extra credit, share a thought or topic online that you are going to apply your new practice of "Cancel. Surrender. Release. Allow."

cancel
surrender
release
allow

"But those who hope in the Lord will renew their strength. They will soar on wings like eagles; they will run and not grow weary, they will walk and not be faint."

– ISAIAH 40:31

THE EAGLE HAS LANDED

Heading out from the conference, I loaded up my Jeep with the four-foot eagle painting and hit the road back home to Detroit. It barely fit in the car. As I began to drive, I knew exactly what to do with this painting. It was going to be a gift to my best friend, Jobie.

Jobie is one of those guys that would give you the shirt off his back. He's loyal, hardworking, and an incredible family man. His family is family to us. It also helps that our wives our best friends, too. We have learned so much from Jobie and his wife, particularly about raising children. Their family is extra full with 5 incredible boys who could field a hockey team. We admire and love them so much.

Our love for Jobie goes so deep that when our son was born we decided to name him after him. Shown above is a picture of Uncle Jobie holding baby Jobie. I love seeing how proud he is as he holds his namesake.

Two years after that picture was taken, Uncle Jobie entered the hardest season of his life.

A Season of Trials

One of the reasons why I wanted to give Jobie the eagle painting was that it was symbolic for strength and protection – two things that he needed as he was going through a horrific season of health issues. At 40 years old, he was diagnosed out of the blue with a very aggressive form of cancer. As he began to fight for his life, our friendship grew closer than I could have ever imagined. One weekend around the holidays, I decided to drive from Detroit to Pittsburgh to spend some time with him and deliver the eagle painting. During my drive, one thing that kept popping up in my mind was to sit closely with him and pray together. This was a bit strange because we had never done this sort of thing before.

Once I arrived at his house, I learned that he was upstairs resting after having an intense radiation treatment. As I walked towards his bedroom, I felt nervous as I wasn't sure what to expect. I entered his bedroom door and saw he was lying in his bed. He greeted me with a tired smile, and I quietly said hi and stood next to his bed. We began to talk, and I eventually sat down next to him. I let him know the eagle painting had arrived safely and was waiting for him downstairs. He smiled and said thank you.

As we continued to talk, he sat up in his bed and said, "I have something to tell you." I listened eagerly as he said, "Mark, I really want to work on my relationship with God this weekend." With chills running down my spine, I looked back at him and said, "Me too, Jobie."

After asking him some questions about his faith journey, he shared that he was pretty new to this whole God thing. He felt guilty for not really talking to God in the past and questioned himself for beginning to do so now that he was sick and needed help. I encouraged him to cancel that thought and just begin where he was today. I asked if we could pray together and he said yes.

As I began to pray, I felt God's presence fill the room. I invited him to pray as well. As he began to speak, a flood of tears poured out of him. We sat in silence as we held hands crying together. As we began to talk about what just happened, Jobie asked me if I heard any music while we were praying? I said, "No, did you?" He said that he heard the song 'Away in the Manger' clear as day! I let him know that I didn't hear anything, and he began to smile as tears rolled down his eyes. It was a moment I'll never forget, and it flooded our hearts with a sense of peace like I've never felt before.

The Pathway to Peace

Over that weekend, we committed to walking down the pathway to peace together. This meant that no matter what happened in life, we were going to focus on giving thanks and praise for each day. We also felt an unspoken

vow to face every challenge together. Over the next 18 months, Jobie faced many challenges. As each challenge entered his pathway, it made him stronger in faith and character. It also continued to form an unbreakable bond in our friendship.

As we both reflect on this crazy journey, Jobie reminds me of the amazing team of support he's had in his corner, including the eagle who has brought him strength and protection everyday.

As I reflect on his words, I feel grateful knowing that 'the eagle has landed' to its rightful owner and will continue to soar with us both down the pathway to peace for the rest of our lives.

COURAGE TO CONNECT OFFLINE

Think of a time in your life that you were faced with trials. Write down what comes to mind below and how these trials have helped shaped your life.

COURAGE TO CONNECT ONLINE

Think about someone that you've seen online that is dealing with a traumatic life event. It could be a health issue, a season of loss, or a struggle that has them feeling down and out. Write the name of this person below, and then write down a creative way that you can connect with them this week. It could be inviting them to go for a walk, meeting up for a cup of coffee, or sending them a direct message online inviting them to connect on a call. Whatever comes to mind, write it down below.

"I've learned that people will forget what you said, people will forget what you did, but people will never forget how you made them feel."

— MAYA ANGELOU

AN EXTRAORDINARY MAN

There was nothing ordinary about Tim Smith.

He was often seen in a Mickey Mouse t-shirt, wearing a flannel paired with nice dress shoes. He idolized Bill Murray (before anyone else did). He owned every Prince album ever produced and rode around town on a pink bicycle encouraging people to Dare Mighty Things!

One may find these things unusual for a 54-year-old man. Personally, I find them remarkable. Tim's most remarkable qualities were best reflected in Skidmore Studio's core values (Be Creative, Challenge, Team, Communication, Integrity, Details and Enjoy).

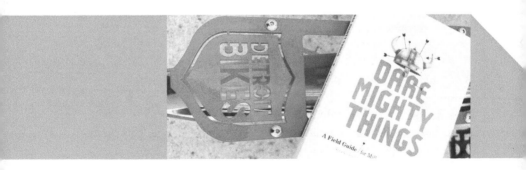

Pictured above, you'll find him standing proudly behind a pet project he crafted over a long weekend. Like a young man eager to show his parents something he'd built, Tim stood tall as he walked our team through the importance of each value and its meaning to him. At the end of his remarks, our core values came to life via the wooden block figure shown above.

An Emotional Leader

Tim wore his emotions on his sleeve and would often tear up at our team meetings. He cared so deeply about the people he worked with and the values we all shared. Each time he got emotional, the same sequence of events would happen:

1. His forehead would begin to sweat.

2. His hands would have a subtle shake.

3. And his glasses would come off (as demonstrated above).

Like a catcher behind home base, you knew when the fastball of tears was bound to come across the plate of Tim's heartfelt message. This quality drew you to him. He was real. He was vulnerable. And he was always sincere.

A Life-Size Spirit

One month after the photo was taken above, Tim passed away suddenly from heart complications. It was a shock to his family, the Studio, and the entire Detroit community.

Tim was one of those people that made you feel better just by being around him. Beyond the fact he was my boss, he was a mentor, a friend, and in a strange way, somewhat of a father figure. I know many people that knew him had a similar connection. Now more than ever, our team continues to live out these values as we move Tim's vision to "Create the Extraordinary" into the future.

At Your Core

It's hard to uncover the core of who you are and dig into what you stand for. After all, it's already in you. Spending time to reflect inward on the values that are authentic to you is an important aspect of a meaningful life. Unfortunately, this isn't a regular event on your already busy calendar.

In loving memory of
Timothy Moodey Smith
September 11, 1963 – January 16, 2018

My challenge to you is to find the time to reflect on your core values. Tap into what makes you tick. Let the real you bubble up. Spend time embracing what makes you, you. Only then, can you define and determine your core values.

If you find you need a little help and inspiration along the way, seek out the Tims in your life. They may or may not be riding a pink bike, but their glowing passion for life should be easy to spot. But most of all, find time to be vulnerable and take off your glasses once in a while.

COURAGE TO CONNECT OFFLINE

If someone asked you to describe your core values, would you know what to tell them? One way to find out is to write them down. Take a few minutes and think about the values that you hold. Make a list of as many as you can. Once you have that list written down, circle the top five values that you believe you stand for most. This is a good start to having clarity on your core values.

COURAGE TO CONNECT ONLINE

One way to bring clarity to your values is to determine people you aspire to live like. Think about someone that inspires you. Look them up and send them an email or tag them on social media with a list of reasons how and why they inspire you. If you have the ability, invite this person to do a Zoom call. During the call, ask them what their core values are and what they do to live them out daily.

"Your greatest contribution may not be something you do but someone you raise."

– ANDY STANLEY

A LIVING LEGACY

As I shared in the story, "An Extraordinary Man," Tim Smith was somewhat of a father figure to me. A father himself, Tim has two sons that continue to live out his legacy. I've formed a friendship with them and often share a meal with his youngest son, Harrison.

Like Father Like Son

During one of our meals, I walked into the restaurant and immediately had chills down my spine as I saw Harrison sitting at the same table his dad and I used to sit at.

As we sipped coffee, we talked about life, relationships, faith, philosophy, and of course, his dad. Somewhere along the line, the topic of our families' nationalities came up.

I asked Harrison what nationality he was and without skipping a beat he said proudly, "I'm a Detroiter." I smiled ear-to-ear thinking, "This is exactly what his dad would have said."

As we ordered our food, I prompted him to go first.

He looked over the menu and with an eager voice said to the waitress, "I'll have the caboose."

I thought to myself, "What the heck is the caboose?"

A quick glance down the menu and boom – there it was! The perfect blend of corn beef, hash browns, eggs and toast (as shown above).

As I ordered my two eggs scrambled with a side of avocado, I noticed Harrison looking at me the same way his dad would have in the past when we had shared a meal. It was the look of "What a lame choice for a greasy spoon diner!" Prompted by his body language, I threw in a side of cinnamon raisin bread to toughen up my order. :)

My Plate and Heart Were Full

During our meal I felt an array of feelings flowing through my heart, with the primary one being joy. In a strange way, part of me felt like I was sharing one more meal with his dad. Between his mannerisms, smile, and big round glasses, it was obvious why I felt this way. However, the other part of me felt thankful for my friendship with Harrison.

As much as he reminded me of Tim, he is also clearly his own person – one who is coming off a really rough year and ready to make small shifts towards a New Year filled with new adventures. It was inspiring to be with him.

There was no doubt in my mind that the legacy Tim left is alive in Harrison. And it is also shining back at Skidmore Studio, the creative company that Tim previously owned.

A Toast to Tim

I learned so much from Tim, as did countless people that knew him. As we celebrated his life back at the studio, we toasted over whiskey and a few tears.

We reflected on many memories and talked about things like:

- His ability to make you feel like part of his family.

- His unshakeable devotion and love for his wife, Colleen.

- His love and pride for his boys, Harrison and Hayden.

- His big heart, full of big ideas.

- His struggle to follow through on his big ideas. :)

- His love for baseball.

- The incredible book he wrote the year before he passed, *Dare Mighty Things*.

- The core values he knitted into the fabric of the studio.

- His love and passion for the City of Detroit.

- The Dr. Seuss book that guided his career, *Oh, The Places You Will Go*.

- And so much more...

In between stories, there was a common feeling people expressed of how they felt his spirit through various signs and serendipitous happenings. Drew Patrick, our new owner and longtime friend and business partner of Tim's, put it perfectly. With confidence in his voice and tears in his eyes he said, "I know Tim's looking down on us smiling. I can feel that he's happy. I can feel that he's proud of us."

Living Your Legacy

You don't have to own a company. You don't need to have children. And you don't have to write a book or be from Detroit, either. You just need to be you. Make memories with those you love most and embrace all of the ways that make you, you. Try each day to enjoy your life and the gifts you've been given. And try your best to do good, for that's ultimately the only thing you can control. If you approach each day with this mindset, chances are you will create a living legacy like Tim's that gives back for generations to come.

COURAGE TO CONNECT OFFLINE

Have you ever thought about what your legacy stands for? One way to do that is to write your own eulogy. I know this sounds a bit morbid, but if you view this exercise as a way to express the things you desire your life to stand for, it can be a very powerful experience. Grab a pen and write out the words you hope your life stands for when your time has come to pass.

COURAGE TO CONNECT ONLINE

Mentorship is a powerful way to create connection. Mentors can often provide counsel and insight into the direction of your life. Take some time and reach out to a few people that you desire to connect with. Ask them if they would consider being your mentor. Let them know that you just want to reach out to them from time to time for their counsel and advice. See if you can set up a standing Zoom call with them.

"Faith is taking the first step even when you don't see the whole staircase."

— MARTIN LUTHER KING, JR.

CREATED FOR GREATNESS

This story is not about doing more, it's about *seeing* more – seeing the way that you are created for greatness and building your faith that this vision will one day come to fruition.

Building Your Faith

Faith is a very personal thing. Faith is the sum total of everything you put your trust in. Not everyone shares the same views or holds the same beliefs, which is why we are all on our own journey!

The more clarity you have concerning your unique identity, the more you will be able to understand your purpose and make it clearer on how you utilize the greatness that lies within you. Often, we aren't clear on the vision we want for our life, which can leave us feeling foggy regarding our future.

Following the Nudges

Take a moment and think about the things that put a fire in your belly and maybe even make you feel a little nervous about pursuing. When you think about these things, do you ever notice a quiet little nudge that's encouraging you act on them? Often, these nudges prompt questions like: "Am I able to do such a thing? Do I deserve this? How would that be possible?"

Below are three quick examples where I've followed nudges that I've been given, even when I felt those same doubting questions:

1. Purchasing the exact home, we live in today.

2. Becoming a professional speaker and author.

3. Singing my wedding vows to my wife. ;-)

Each vision started with a thought, led to a burning desire, and eventually came to life. The key is to stand faithfully in the vision you see in your mind and cast out any anxiety and fear of where you are today. The difference from your current state to your envisioned state is called 'The Gap.'

Many people lose sight of a vision or fold into fear in the gap. The power of standing in the gap and seeing the vision into reality is where the magic happens.

Now I know that some of you may be rolling your eyes in doubt. I have some good news: 'visioning' is a skill you can learn! By creating a vision, you can have a significant impact on building your faith all while helping to see how you are made for greatness.

Learning the Art of Visioning

I had an opportunity to go through a two-day intensive training on Creating A Vision of Greatness. This was put on through ZingTrain, an extraordinary training company that is part of the Zingerman's family of companies out of Ann Arbor, Michigan. Pictured above is the co-founder, Ari Weinzweig, who has built his business and culture on the process of visioning.

One of the main elements to learning the skill of visioning is to create your future with as much detail as possible! These details include all of the five senses. For example, "What does your new job feel like? What does the cover of your book you want to write look like? How does the meal taste that you've prepared in your dream kitchen? What is the smell of your newborn baby like?"

Spare no details in your vision. Feel it. See it. Believe it to be true! The art of practicing visioning is a learned behavior and over time will create clarity in your life.

20/20 Vision

As you reflect on your goals and vision, take your skills, interests, desires and get going! Start writing them down, get hyper specific, and even invest in a visioning book and/or training. Stand in the gap of where you are today and have faith in the vision of your future self. **You are a masterpiece created for greatness**!

COURAGE TO CONNECT OFFLINE

Do you have a clear vision for what it is you want to pursue and achieve? Take a few minutes and reflect on this question. Feel free to jot down any thoughts in the area below.

COURAGE TO CONNECT ONLINE

Google "Visioning and Ari Weinzweig." Read through the details on "How to Create A Vision." This may serve as motivation for you to craft your own vision!

"Setting goals is the first step in turning the invisible into the visible."

— TONY ROBBINS

MAKE TIME TO WRITE DOWN YOUR GOALS

Every year my wife and I spend an afternoon together writing down our goals and manifesting the future that we want for our family and ourselves.

We've learned to reflect on the things we desire and take time to thoughtfully write them down. Words have power and when written down, they can become your reality. However, your goals can fall apart if you are unable to defeat the distractions that prevent you from accomplishing them.

Don't Repeat Last Year's Distractions

Before you craft your goals for the New Year, I suggest you reflect on the things that distracted you from accomplishing your previous year's goals. It will come to no surprise that social media and cell phone use top the list.

According to research aggregated by Medikix, below is the **average time spent per day** across the most popular social media sites in 2016:

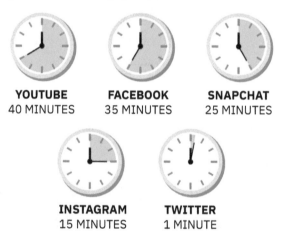

YOUTUBE
40 MINUTES

FACEBOOK
35 MINUTES

SNAPCHAT
25 MINUTES

INSTAGRAM
15 MINUTES

TWITTER
1 MINUTE

Add these minutes over the course of the year and your jaw may drop! Below are the total hours per year the average user spends on each site:

YouTube = 240 hours

Facebook = 213 hours

Snapchat = 152 hours

Instagram = 91 hours

Twitter = 6 hours

Even if you are only on Facebook, you spend upwards of 200+ hours per year on social media! Don't believe me? In an article by the *New York Times*, Facebook has 50 minutes of your time each day, and it wants more.

Just imagine how far you could advance your goals by redirecting your time to something more productive. Here are a few examples to inspire you for this upcoming year:

1. Read a 300-page book in ten hours.

2. Train for a half marathon in 28 hours.

3. Learn Spanish in 480 hours.

4. Become a basic guitar player in 120 hours.

And these are just a few thought starters!

Digging Deeper

How long do you think it takes to repair a relationship with a loved one? How about the self-care required to heal the emotional pain you've been holding onto for the past decade? Or breaking that habit you know isn't good for you? All of these things require an intentionality that is best cultivated by spending time reflecting and writing – not scrolling and liking.

Your time is precious. There is no app, no post, and no amount of virtual attention that can replace the benefit of investing time towards goals that advance your emotional, physical, and spiritual health.

My Challenge to You!

Invest time in passions and people that matter most to you.

Travel beyond fake news and edited moments portrayed online.

Begin to thrive in an environment created first in your mind, then on paper, and eventually in the world around you.

Anything is possible, you just need to write down your goals!

COURAGE TO CONNECT OFFLINE

Make a list of three goals that you want to focus on in the following 90 days. Write them down below.

COURAGE TO CONNECT ONLINE

Make a commitment to share the progress of your goals online. This can be a great way to hold yourself accountable while having people encourage the advancements of your goals.

"It's easy to stand in the crowd, but it takes courage to stand alone."

– MAHATMA GANDHI

FEELING LONELY?

Taking care of children may be the hardest job on earth. I've had the chance to spend some solo dad time with our kids as my wife headed out for various photo shoots (she's a gifted photographer). The day would start off with smiles and laughs as shown below,

but as the morning went on, I found my sanity melting away as each hour that passed felt like an entire day! Between nap schedules, making bottles, temper tantrums, soiled bed sheets, and Amazon Prime deliveries (which always come at nap time and triggered the dogs to bark) I felt like I was going insane.

During any moments of downtime, I found myself turning to my phone to catch a glimpse into the outside world. It went beyond checking social media and email. I found myself checking Slack, my company's internal messaging system for project updates, lunchtime banter, and random Gifs that made their way into the rhythm of the work day – anything that gave me a sense of connection!

Facebook, Instagram, and the Obituaries?

Although a quick glance at Facebook or Instagram appears to fill the social void of adult interaction, it often leads to feelings of envy and increased loneliness. I recently asked my mom for perspective on what she would do when feeling exhausted and overdue for some social connection while raising four kids in the 1980's. Her response was telling.

She would reach for the newspaper and read the obituaries.

Yes. The obituaries!

She went on to say that it made her feel better because she knew that she was alive – even if she was juggling the needs of three toddlers and a baby!

At first I found this strange. Then I quickly realized it's really no different than what motivates us to check our phone. We crave connection. We seek attention. We need human interaction. We were designed for real relationships. But it's not just stay-at-home parents that can feel lonely. The corporate workplace is also showing signs of loneliness.

So Why Are We So Lonely?

Sherry Turkle, Professor at MIT and author of *Alone Together* says it best:

"Technology promises to let us do anything from anywhere with anyone. But it also drains us as we try to do everything everywhere. We begin to feel overwhelmed and depleted by the lives technology makes possible. We may be free to work from anywhere, but we are also prone to being lonely everywhere."

Another great example of Turkle's work can be seen in a video called, "The Innovation of Loneliness." I highly recommend you Google it.

Ways to Combat Loneliness

Although checking the obituaries seems like an odd way to combat loneliness, the act of picking up the paper and reading the death notices probably takes a sum total of five minutes.

In today's scrollable world, it's easy to spend countless hours hoping to find meaningful connection in our day. And the more we scroll, the less likely we are to find time to be in relationship with those around us. Deep down inside I know there is a way for us to truly find connection beyond our screens. Here are a few suggestions to combat loneliness:

- Seek involvement in community (join a small group, engage in mentorship, start volunteering).
- Take a staycation or a couple days off of work to reset.

- Skip the email or text – call a friend!

- Find someone to talk to (a therapist, a family member, co-worker, etc.).

Whichever ways you choose to combat loneliness, there's a good chance it will have a positive impact on you and on someone else – which is a great way to start making a shift in the loneliness epidemic. And for those parents out there, be present with your children and put down the phone – especially while changing diapers!

COURAGE TO CONNECT OFFLINE

When you are feeling lonely, you need to establish an action plan that will help you get out of your own way. Take some time and write down five things to do when you are feeling lonely. The next time you find yourself looking for community, come back to this list and pick something from it to do.

COURAGE TO CONNECT ONLINE

The next time you are feeling lonely or restless and you aren't sure what you are going to do with your time, pick up your phone and call a friend. See if they are open for a FaceTime or Zoom call, even if you are just calling to say, "Hi!" for five minutes.

"Nothing diminishes anxiety faster than action."

– WALTER ANDERSON

START TODAY

For the past few months my wife has suggested I read the book *Girl Stop Apologizing* by Rachel Hollis. After much resistance (for obvious reasons), I finally decided to listen to the first chapter. I'm glad I did.

Hollis writes about creating a 'shame-free' plan to focus on your dreams and desires without worrying about what other people think. She encourages you to stop apologizing for what you are trying to accomplish and just go do it!

I've learned in life that this requires us to cut through the mounting resistance that blocks our minds from taking action on things we know we need to do. Although seemingly straightforward, this is no small feat.

The Power of Resistance

Resistance often tries to take up residence in my mind. But it's not always my dreams that I'm resisting. It's the work I need to do on myself that often slows me down the most. Here are a few examples:

- It took me ten years of struggling with seasonal depression to finally reach out to a therapist. And it took me three therapists to find the right one, which added to the already compounding resistance!

- Even though writing stories is often on my heart, it can be a struggle to get them down on paper. Doubt always creeps in (resistance's best friend) and makes me wonder if people really even care about what I have to say?

- Getting up early in the morning when I'm overtired and don't want to deal with the kids can trigger a tap of the snooze button on my alarm clock. This tendency eliminates my extra time to work towards my dreams.

I could share a dozen more ways resistance has delayed my aspirations and goals. Instead, I'll share two simple words that can kick resistance out of your life: Start Today.

Start Today

A dear friend of ours gifted my wife and I each a journal that Rachel Hollis created to help promote gratitude and making your dreams happen. The journal is appropriately called *Start Today*. It begins with a writing exercise to help you see your future self. Once this foundation is established, you write daily based on the simple but powerful template at right.

I've been writing in it daily. It helps me realize that the only way I'm going to fight through the resistance that comes with each day is to just start! Start by taking action. Start by writing things down. Start today.

If Not Now, Then When?

I know what you're thinking – "Sounds like a good idea, Mark. I'm just going to wait and get started on this once my *<insert reason here>* happens."

The problem with this answer is that it fosters resistance. By starting today, you will strengthen the muscle in your mind that builds character and self-confidence. So I ask you, "If Not Now, Then When?"

BTW, my wife has this exact saying framed in our kitchen helping to remind us daily to take action. It helps keep us focused and reminds us to *Start Today!*

DATE:

TODAY I AM GRATEFUL FOR:

1. _____
2. _____
3. _____
4. _____
5. _____

TEN DREAMS I MADE HAPPEN:

1. _____
2. _____
3. _____
4. _____
5. _____
6. _____
7. _____
8. _____
9. _____
10. _____

THE GOAL I AM GOING TO ACHIEVE FIRST:

COURAGE TO CONNECT OFFLINE

What is preventing you from taking action? What lie has resistance been speaking to you? Take a moment and reflect on what comes to mind and write it down below.

COURAGE TO CONNECT ONLINE

There are wonderful ways to connect in community online. You can join a Facebook group for writers, musicians, chefs, and other aspiring interests. Identify what it is you are looking to follow through on and find an online community to join.

"If you change the way you look at things, the things you look at change."

— WAYNE DYER

ARE YOU RESTORABLE?

We recently decided to restore an old fountain by planting flowers in it. Our kids were so excited to lend a hand. They put on their sun hats, grabbed a step stool, and began to get their hands dirty. It was precious! Our three-year-old daughter attempted to dig the soil deep enough while holding the fragile petunias in her little hands. A few flower petals broke off and fell to the ground as she continued along confidently. Although her planting techniques weren't perfect, it was a perfect sight to witness.

My son also enjoyed getting his hands dirty and helping restore the fountain back to life. They took turns planting flowers while I stood back supervising. As I watched this old fountain transform into a beautiful flower bed, I began to feel full of joy.

My wife came outside and celebrated our teamwork and let us know that dinner was ready. We planted the last flower and went inside, feeling accomplished and hungry for the delicious meal she cooked up.

What Happened Next

As the kids washed up, I went outside to quickly clean up. I marveled at the finished product while touching up a couple of loose ends. All of a sudden, the entire fountain collapsed! It literally crumbled before my eyes.

In what felt like slow motion, my eyes watched the head of the statue break off as it hit the ground. The incredibly heavy coy fish-shaped base split in two, dumping the clamshell flower bed exactly where my daughter had stood just a few minutes earlier!

The joy I had previously felt turned into immediate sadness. I walked back inside, and with a somber tone I shared the news to the family. My wife and I looked at each other knowing that the sentimental fountain was no longer going to be part of our daily view.

As we reflected on what just happened, we felt the peace of God come over us as we focused on the fact that nobody got hurt. The fountain was so heavy that it could have crushed our kids and severely hurt them. We ate dinner discussing what just happened as I wondered how we were going to clean up the aftermath.

Restoration Round 2

We went back outside and our neighbors came over to help. We all stood around the fountain and began to rethink how we could salvage the remnants. As the sun began to set, we landed on a plan on how to restore it. We lifted the clamshell together while placing it where the coy fish used to sit. The girls began to re-plant the flowers, while the guys began to break up the rest of the fountain with a sledgehammer. It was the ideal division of labor!

We glued the head back on the statue and laced the base of the new setup with commercial grade concrete glue. Before too long, what appeared to be a lost cause was taking on a whole new form. The kids celebrated as the new fountain took shape, and the adults began to feel the accomplishment of working together. Our restoration project was complete!

Final Reflections

How often do you look at something or someone as broken and unfixable? I feel that life is full of opportunities to reflect on what we need to restore. You may need to reset your expectations on what something *was* and focus on a healthy view of what *is*. And if you need to break out your sledgehammer, make sure to wear your safety glasses as pieces of the past are sure to fly around you!

COURAGE TO CONNECT OFFLINE

Think about something in your life that needs to be restored. It could be a relationship, a flawed perspective within yourself, or even an old item around your house. Write down what comes to mind including one way you can begin to restore it.

COURAGE TO CONNECT ONLINE

Find something around your house that you can restore over a weekend. Now post the before and after photos online and share something that you learned during your restoration experience!

"You can't pour from an empty cup. Take care of yourself first."

— UNKNOWN

RESOURCES

The following resources are intended to
encourage a spirit of digital wellness in
your life. These resources are meant
as suggestions, not requirements. May
they remind you that relationships are
designed to be relational in nature through
warm-blooded connections, not just
transactional through cold-blooded devices.

"**Almost everything will work again if you unplug it for a few minutes, including you.**"

– ANNE LAMOTT

10
SIGNS YOU NEED A BREAK FROM YOUR PHONE

Do you know the word "nomophobia"? It is a term describing a growing fear in today's world – the fear of being without a mobile device or beyond mobile phone contact. Here are a few staggering statistics that highlight just how extreme this can be:

- Sixty-five percent, or about two out of three people, sleep with or next to their smartphones.

- One in five people would rather go without shoes for a week than take a break from their phone.

- More than half never switch off their phone.

- Thirty-four percent admitted to answering their cell phone during intimacy with their partner.

- A full 66 percent of all adults suffer from "nomophobia."

Personally, I check my phone upwards of 100 times a day. It's exhausting. I often refer to it as the Holy Trinity of checking: work email (Father), personal Gmail (Son), and then Facebook (the Holy Spirit). I know I'm not alone.

Nomophobia is a real thing that has a significant impact on the very nature of our existence. I believe this dependence on our devices is compromising our mental, physical, and spiritual health. Following are ten signs that you may be suffering from nomophobia and need a break from your phone.

1. You hide in the bathroom to check your phone. Not sure if this one is just for parents of young children, but I find myself extending my own bathroom breaks in hopes to escape the temper tantrum and poopy diaper that awaits me. If you don't have kids, consider this – when was the last time you went to the bathroom without your phone?

2. You're too tired to be intimate but can lay in bed for an hour on Instagram. Thankfully, I can't relate to this one, but I have heard this from multiple audience members. A woman in her mid 20's stated, "I just want to be left alone so I can go to bed and enjoy Instagramming by myself."

3. You get honked at every time the light turns green. Looking down at your phone during a red light isn't texting and driving, right? Wrong. Even though it doesn't seem as bad, there is a good chance that if you're scrolling at a red light, you're scrolling going 80 miles per hour down the highway.

4. You have aches and pains in places you didn't know could hurt. You wonder why your neck always hurts. You're convinced you have a bum thumb. Your eyes burn and your migraine is back. Rx = Take three days off your device and call me in the morning. XOXO, Dr. Obvious.

5. You can't put down your phone. Just-one-more-text. You started the day with your phone, you've brought it to the bathroom, you've driven it to work, you've placed it next to your fork at dinner time. Heck, you've even set it on your butt for the better part of the day. You're fighting exhaustion, yet your phone is always with you.

6. Your doctor has the same last name as a search engine. Who needs a doctor when you have Google? Aside from the fact that you've misdiagnosed yourself with the measles, bird flu, and other fatal illnesses all within the last six months.

7. Your 30-minute workout isn't 'working out' so well. You spent the first 15 minutes trying to find that perfect Pandora channel to pump-you-up. The remaining time was spent doing reps of texting, checking email, and the occasional phone call.

8. You realize group texts aren't as fun as hanging with friends. It's 11:00 p.m. at night and you're climbing into bed. One of your friends sends a group text to a dozen people. You try your hardest to ignore it and even think about using the "Do Not Disturb" feature. You opt to head to bed instead and enjoy a broken night's sleep with annoying notifications drifting in your dreams.

9. You wish you had more time for hobbies. If only there were more time in the day. Oh wait, what about the 160 times that you checked your phone today? Add that time up over the course of the week and you may find a couple extra hours to dabble in that craft you've been longing to take up.

10. You've written a poem about your phone. Okay, this one may just be for me. But while I'm on the topic, take a minute and check out this love ballad I wrote for my phone titled, "Disconnect Me" at markostach.com/spoken-word/.

COURAGE TO CONNECT OFFLINE

When is the last time you've taken a digital fast from your phone? Pick one hour today that you will put your phone on airplane mode. Or better yet, pick one hour that you will leave your phone in your house while you go outside of your house to run an errand or go for a walk. As you take a digital fast for one hour, reflect on how you are feeling. If you build up enough courage, try applying that one-hour-fast principal to the rest of the week!

COURAGE TO CONNECT ONLINE

Announcing that you are going to take a fast from social media is like telling people you are never going to drink again when you wake up with a hangover. People don't believe you! And you probably don't believe yourself. Instead of announcing your break from social media, just take a full day, or better yet, take a whole week. The reality is, people aren't really going to notice if you take a few days off. It's like leaving a party and not saying goodbye to anyone — you are the only person that truly needs to know you've left.

"The most productive things we can do is stop working on someone else's task list."

– SETH GODIN

5
WAYS TO PREVENT EMAIL OVERLOAD

Do you skim through emails without fully reading them? Feel like you can never catch up on unread or flagged messages? You're not alone.

I'd like to offer up a few ways to be more productive with your communication and provide some relief from your never-ending inbox.

I Know What You're Thinking...

Email is the lifeline of your business. Your team depends on your ability to respond to them. This is how your clients reach you. Heck, you already have 18 unread emails, and it's not even 10.00 a.m.! *Slow-down. Take a deep breath.* I'm not saying to stop email altogether. However, I do want to point out a few reasons why you should reconsider email as your primary mode of communication.

Three Reasons to Reconsider

1. **People are overloaded.** We are beyond the era of information overload. We need the jaws of life to set us free. Between flooded inboxes and fake news, it's becoming hard to determine what's important and what's not.

2. **TLDR.** Too Long Didn't Read. People don't have time to read. They don't even have time to go grocery shopping (#InstaCart). If you find yourself starting a sentence with "Lastly,...." I can assure you that the email wasn't read.

3. **F-You email.** I'm not mad at email. I'm just pointing out what science is telling us about the way we read. Our eyes follow text on the screen in the form of the letter F. We start by reading the top line, then scroll down and read halfway through, and swiftly scan to the end of the page like an anchor hitting the bottom of the ocean. All this in the form of the letter F.

Five Ways to Better Connect

I've learned that forming and fostering connections rarely comes just from email alone. Here are five additional suggestions on how you can better connect with the people you work with:

1. **Pick up the phone**. Try it. It's amazing how often you'll reach the person you need to get a hold of. In order to do this, you'll need to break the habit of hiding behind the screen. Just remember this: CBE = Call Before Email!

2. **Send a text prior to 8.30 a.m.** Before the chaos of the day gets going, try sending a text early in the morning. If you need a quick response, you may be able to catch the person during their cup of coffee or morning routine.

3. **Use a scheduling tool.** Asking someone for their time can be a game of chess. And finding time that works for both sides can be exhausting. Avoid these moments by using a scheduling tool like Calendly or Doodle to save precious time and energy.

4. **Send snail mail.** Nothing beats getting a handwritten note from someone. There's mutual gratitude and appreciation exchanged when writing or receiving a piece of mail. It takes time, but it's well worth the investment.

5. **Touch their hand.** Okay, not literally, but sort of. Spend time face-to-face with your clients and team. This is how you get to know each other. This is how relationships are built.

Be Bold. Break the Cycle.

Sending email has become the new norm to our workforce. Step out of your inbox and into a moment of courage to break the cycle of email overload. Your clients and team will thank you.

COURAGE TO CONNECT OFFLINE

Search through your email and find someone that you email regularly but rarely see (if ever) in person. If possible, give that person a call and invite them to share a meal or a cup of coffee. If that isn't possible, write them a thank-you card. Share with them why you appreciate them. BTW, don't email them and say "I've sent you something in the mail." Just let them be surprised by your snail mail when it arrives.

COURAGE TO CONNECT ONLINE

If your job allows, dedicate two times during the day to check your email, once in the morning and once in the afternoon. There are dozens of articles that show how learning a productive way to manage email will allow for deep thinking and creativity to flow from your day when email is parked in the background.

"A vacation is what you take when you can no longer take what you've been taking."

— EARL WILSON

10

BENEFITS OF TAKING AN EMAIL VACATION

When is the last time you took a long weekend away from your phone? How do you think your time would be if you didn't check your email?

I tested this out myself on a long weekend my family and I had together. I made a vow to myself that I wouldn't check email for the entire week, and I'm proud to say that I stuck to that vow. I didn't check my email for seven full days. Not even once. As I look back on this experience, I'd like to share a few reflections and offer several tips that can help you stay off email during your next vacation (or long weekend away).

My Motivation

Two kids, two dogs, and enough supplies to last a month. After a last-minute Amazon Prime purchase of a soft top carrier for the van, we packed everyone in and began our journey to Lake Michigan.

It was the first official trip with the entire family. Our daughter was five-months old and our son was about to be three. Spending quality time together was my main goal. Key word being "quality."

I spend plenty of time with my wife and kids. However, it's not always quality time. This is often due to my impulse to check my email, which shifts my attention to work as opposed to being present with them. As an added element of motivation, I wanted to test my willpower. Sounds crazy, but coming from someone who teaches people how to create healthy digital habits, I've often resorted to an app or piece of technology to help out. But this time was different. I scheduled my "Out-Of-Office" message, set expectations with my team and clients, and never looked back (or down for that matter).

Ten Immediate Benefits

I experienced several benefits by not checking email while on vacation including:

1. I was less irritable.
2. I was more patient.
3. I laughed more.
4. I wasn't always thinking about work.
5. I processed (not just listened) to what my wife was saying. :)
6. My morning routine was lifted through reading books (i.e. *Utmost for His Highest, Minute of Margin*).
7. I slept better, and I didn't have random stressful dreams.
8. I felt more present.
9. I was less stressed and enjoyed my time away from work.
10. I was refreshed and ready to get back into work.

You'll Feel Better

Studies show that taking time off from work – and work-related email – lowers levels of fatigue and job burnout. Employees who come back rested tend to perform better at solving problems and other creative tasks.

Inspired by an article in the *Harvard Business Review*, a friend of mine recently sent an email to his team with the subject line: "Make Not Working Part of Work."

He stated it was just as important to disconnect from the office and take time off as any other project the team was working on.

He also suggested that people leave their "Out-Of-Office" response on for one additional day after their scheduled vacation so that they could catch up on email and reduce the stress that comes from being away from work.

You'll Never Know Unless You Try

Trust me. The benefits of going a long weekend without checking email will pay dividends to your mind, body, and spirit. Give it a whirl; you have nothing to lose and so much to gain.

COURAGE TO CONNECT OFFLINE

Turn off or remove your email from your phone before leaving for vacation. Let someone know what you are doing and why you are choosing to do this. This person will act as your accountability partner to help keep you off of email!

COURAGE TO CONNECT ONLINE

Here is a great "Out-Of-Office" template that you can use to help foster the benefits of taking time off from checking email while you enjoy some fun in the sun!

Hello!

I'll be recharging with some time away from work and won't be checking my email while I'm away. I'll return on <u>date</u>. If you need anything while I'm away, please contact <u>team member name</u> at <u>555-555-555</u> or <u>team-member@ companyname.com</u>.

Looking forward to coming back refreshed and ready to respond to your email!

<u>*Your Name*</u>

P.S. Check out the benefits to staying off email while away from work:

Studies show that taking time off from work — and work-related email — lowers levels of fatigue and job burnout. Employees who come back rested tend to perform better at solving problems and other creative tasks.

"Health is a state of mind. Wellness is a state of being."

— UNKNOWN

5
WAYS TO
IMPROVE
YOUR DIGITAL
WELLNESS

BY MARK OSTACH   137

Becoming digitally fit is becoming a focus for many. As the need to manage our digital lives becomes more pressing, I'd like to share five tips to help curb poor digital habits while freeing up time for you to focus on what matters most: your own health and well-being.

Below are Five Ways to Improve Your Digital Wellness:

1. **No digital gadgets at meal time.** We have our knives, forks, spoons, and phones! It seems that our dinner tables and mealtimes are a safe place for these devices. Rest assured, there is a better way. When you remove the devices from meal times, you open up the opportunity for conversations and connections. You also become more conscious of the food you are eating and give yourself the chance to digest the physical calories without the empty digital calories that make their way into your mind when often aimlessly scrolling and eating.

2. **Take a digital fast for one hour a day.** Taking a digital fast can be a great baby step at creating healthy space from your device. For me, I choose 6 p.m. to 7 p.m. each day when I'm done with work. This allows me to be focused on my family. For you, it may mean that this time is used to go on a walk or exercise. Whatever you choose, just make sure you pick the same time every day. It will help to make it a habit!

3. **Sleep device free – get a real alarm clock.** Most people use their phones as an alarm clock. Although convenient, this ensures that you

check your phone right when you wake up in the morning. This can flood your mind with panic and To Dos before you've brushed your teeth. Do me a favor – go online and purchase an alarm clock. I recommend a product called Bagby.com that gives you a real alarm clock and a bed for your phone.

4. **End your digital day one hour before bed.** Have you ever been on an airplane? Could you imagine if the pilot tried to drop the plane down for landing 30,000 feet in the air as opposed to descending it onto the runway? The same holds true for landing your body into your bed. Take time to unwind from the screen and descend into peace and quiet. This may include reading a physical book, meditation, or prayer. Regardless of what you choose, just make sure it's without a screen.

5. **Make eye contact when talking.** Have you heard the saying, "Your eyes are the gateway to your soul?" Have you heard the saying, "Your forehead is the gateway to your forehead?" My guess is that you probably haven't heard that. Your forehead doesn't provide any non-verbal cues for the person communicating with you. Take time to put your phone down and make eye contact when talking. It's one of the best gifts you can offer someone.

Bonus Tip: Go Outside and Get Some Fresh Air!

Fresh air is a great way to reset your mind and get your body moving. These are key things to do when we are feeling burnout from screen time. A 15-minute walk around the block can do wonders in renewing your mindset and put you in a better state of mind the next time you go to connect online or in offline conversations.

What People Are Saying

When I speak to groups about digital wellness, I challenge the audience to focus on these tips for the next few weeks and report back to me how they feel. Here are a handful of responses:

• My mindset changes when I put my phone down after work. It relaxes me and frees me to be myself again.

- Since not using my phone all the time, I've gotten closer to the people around me.

- I'm connecting more with my spouse.

- I've noticed that my vocal communication skills have gotten better. I used to hide behind texting. Now I speak up without the use of texting all the time.

- Life is short. I don't want my memories to be filled with looking down at a screen. I now focus on finding new hobbies to replace browsing on social media when I'm bored.

What I'm learning

We are all aware of our physical, emotional, spiritual, and financial health areas of life that we need to work on. However, I'm also learning that people are craving ways to improve their digital health. You have a chance right now to begin taking baby steps in improving your digital health. Trust me, you'll be glad you did so!

COURAGE TO CONNECT OFFLINE

Here's my challenge to you: Pick a habit to focus on and ask a friend or family member to be your digital well-being accountability partner. For a physical printout to help guide you, visit www.markostach.com.

COURAGE TO CONNECT ONLINE

Share how you've felt since you've worked on the digital habit you've selected. Take a few minutes and share on social media and let people know what you've gained by improving your digital wellness.

"Technology
should improve
your life...
not become
your life."

– BILLY COX

5 WAYS TO CREATE A CULTURE OF DIGITAL WELL-BEING

During the Apple Developers Conference in 2019, they announced that the new iOS will have settings that focus on your digital health. This announcement comes in the wake of Google's latest Android updates that focus on digital well-being. Beyond these two leaders, there are other organizations embracing a culture of digital wellness.

- Anheuser-Busch uses beer crates to hold cell phones to promote focused meetings.

- Quicken Loans offers a mobile meditation experience to encourage mindfulness during the work day.

- Thrive Global is on a mission to end the stress and burnout epidemic through positive content and resources.

But you don't have to wait for your company to implement a digital wellness program. You can start by making a few tiny shifts in your workday. Here are five simple ways to help you and encourage your team to embrace a culture of digital well-being.

Five Ways to Create A Culture of Digital Well-being

1. **Establish communication preferences**. In some organizations, there are over four generations working together under one roof. If you prefer that your new intern picks up the phone and calls you and they prefer that you send them a Snapchat, then it's on you to establish your communication preferences.

2. **Set email expectations.** Find yourself catching up on email over the weekends? Be sure to let your team know that this doesn't mean they have to respond. If you haven't let them know this, there's a good chance they are monitoring email on the weekends while they should be making memories with their friends and family!

3. **Start your meetings with something good.** Positive energy attracts positive people. Start by sharing something positive or light hearted. It could be that you had a great workout yesterday, or you recently adopted a dog, or you reconnected with an old friend. It doesn't matter what it is, just make sure it's positive!

4. **Encourage mental breaks.** There's no shortage of research on the benefits of meditation. If you feel intimidated by the idea of meditating, start by taking a five-minute break, close your eyes, and practice some deep breathing. Be sure to put your phone on "Do Not Disturb.";) Have trouble closing your eyes at work? Grab a sheet of paper and write down things you are grateful for. Gratitude helps create a heart filled with joy.

5. **Promote physical activity.** Struggling to find time to exercise? Try squeezing in a quick workout over lunch. And if you plan ahead, you'll pack your lunch, save money, and avoid eating at your desk. Working out over lunch sound impossible? At least take a break and head outside for a lap around your office. Movement and fresh air may give you that burst of energy you need to finish the day strong!

Bonus Tip: Choose Grace over Guilt

Workplace guilt is a silent killer in promoting digital well-being in the workplace. If your job allows you to embrace any of the ideas above, then do it! And if you are feeling guilty about what someone may think, give yourself some grace and go talk to them. Let them know that you are choosing to work on your mental and physical health so that you can be healthier at work. There's a high probability they're also searching for ways to take a break from the screen. They're just looking for someone to help get them motivated!

And remember, no setting on your phone can determine your overall health. The sheer willpower inside of you will determine how you embrace a culture of digital well-being. You can do it!

COURAGE TO CONNECT OFFLINE

Here's my challenge to you: Pick a habit to focus on and ask a co-worker to be your digital well-being accountability partner. See if you can create a way for your team or organization to begin embracing ways to foster digital wellness at work. For a physical printout to help guide you, visit www.markostach.com.

COURAGE TO CONNECT ONLINE

Reach out to someone who has influence in creating change at your organization. This can be your manager, someone in Human Resources, or even the owner of the company. Let them know why you think embracing digital wellness is important and ways you think it can be improved within the company.

"Fatigue makes
fools of us all.
It robs us of
our skills, our
judgement,
and blinds
us to creative
solutions."

– HARVEY MACKAY

5 WAYS TO COMBAT ZOOM FATIGUE

Zoom has quickly become a verb across the globe as the video-conference platform replaces workplaces and schools for easy virtual-meeting setups. As wonderful as Zoom can be, it wasn't intended to replace face-to-face interaction. After back-to-back virtual meetings, we begin to feel exhausted from the constant gaze at our screens. This is when Zoom Fatigue sets in. Our brains experience what's known as *continuous partial attention* where it begins to get tired from continuously paying attention to multiple things at once. Below are five ways that you can combat Zoom Fatigue.

1. **4 x 4 Breathing**. Starting a Zoom meeting can be tricky. People are coming from all directions of the day. Start by doing a 4 x 4 breathing meditation; it only takes a few moments and can bring people into awareness before the purpose of the meeting gets going. Simply ask people to close their eyes and breathe in slowly for four seconds and breathe out slowly for four seconds. Repeat this three more times and watch how people become more present for the start of your Zoom calls.

2. **Stay Confident in the Spotlight!** Have you ever felt like nobody is paying attention to you while you're leading a Zoom meeting? It almost feels like you are on stage with a bright light on your face and nobody is in attendance! Rest assured this isn't the case. Stay focused on your camera and keep smiling! People see and hear you!

3. **Pick Up the Phone**. If it's late in the day and you are feeling Zoomed out, suggest switching the meeting to a standard phone call. Let the

person know that you need a break from video calls and see if they don't mind switching. Most likely, they will be relieved to do so as well.

4. **Keep Structure**. Best practices for in-person meetings have clear goals and an agenda while someone captures next steps. This should hold true for your Zoom meetings as well. Doing so will save time and energy across your team. Side note, for large group meetings or virtual social gatherings, be sure to assign a facilitator.

5. **Moments of Movement**. Our bodies need to move. Stretch, jump, run in place, take a lap around your office, or simply rotate your neck and shoulders. It doesn't matter how you move, it just matters that you make space for movement! Trust me, your teammates will thank you for taking charge and bringing movement into the meeting.

Bonus Tip

Rent a donkey via Zoo Zoom! Zoo Zoom is a new trend where you can rent a farm animal to join your Zoom calls. This is a fun way to add some humor to your meetings.

COURAGE TO CONNECT OFFLINE

Next time you notice that someone appears to be struggling with a personal issue on a Zoom call, pick up the phone and reach out to them after the call. Let them know that you are there for them if they need anything at all.

COURAGE TO CONNECT ONLINE

Try the 4 x 4 breathing exercise on your next Zoom Meeting. Make sure to let people know that you are going to take them through a brief relaxing process that will help them become centered before the meeting begins.

"You can fake a smile, but you can't fake your feelings."

– UNKNOWN

5 BENEFITS TO FEELING YOUR FEELINGS

Our feelings are wisdom to the world around us. For many of us, we don't take time to 'feel our feelings' which impacts our ability to process our emotions. Before we discuss the benefits to feeling our feelings, let's review the three ways we tend to cope with our feelings:

1. **Repress them**. The most common way to deal with our feelings is to repress them. We sweep them under the rug in hopes to one day clean them up. Instead, decades fly by and leave us carrying a whole suitcase full of emotional baggage.

2. **Recycle them.** Recyling our emotions happens when our thoughts begin to cycle around in our head for hours at a time. Like dirty laundry cycling through the washing machine, our worries tumble around while our emotions wash away the fabric of our ability to be present.

3. **Release them**. The best way to deal with our emotions is to release them. When you release your emotions, you acknowledge HOW you are feeling and WHERE the feelings are located in your body. For example, I feel fear in my chest. It's heavy, like a pile of bricks, and is making my shoulders feel tight. Once you are aware of your feelings, you can use movement and sound to release them.

Learning how to release your emotions can take a lifetime to learn. However, those that begin raising their awareness of how to feel and process their feelings can reap many benefits. Below are five benefits to becoming more emotionally intelligent:

1. **Reduce Stress**. Repressing your feelings can lead to stress. Stress manifests itself as physical symptoms like your heart fluttering, your eyelid flickering, or a tension headache. Feeling your emotions and releasing them helps stress to leave the body.

2. **Sleep Better**. The more you sleep, the more likely you are to cope with your emotions. Sleep allows your cells to regenerate and your mind to reset. Those who value sleep create more space to learn, live, and lead with intention.

3. **Build Trust**. Creating meaningful connections with the people on your team is critical to building trust. One way to do that is to ask them a simple question, "How are you feeling?" If they still aren't opening up, ask them a follow up question, "What is the state of your heart?" You'll be surprised how this question will prime them to go deeper in their response.

4. **Heal Your Past**. Dealing with your emotions can help to heal the scars of your past. When we repress difficult seasons of our lives, we may never heal from the lessons these trials were trying to teach us.

5. **Stay Human Centered**. Regardless of your level of success, people want to know that you have struggles, too. Sharing your fears, failures, and feelings with those around you help remind them that you are human, too.

COURAGE TO CONNECT OFFLINE

Take a moment and identify which of the ways you tend to deal with your feelings. Do you repress, recycle, or release them? Write down your response below.

COURAGE TO CONNECT ONLINE

When you see someone posting on social media about a challenging situation they are going through, pick up the phone and simply ask them how they are feeling. Sometimes people just need someone to talk to for a few minutes to make them feel better.

"The key to growth is the introduction of higher dimensions of consciousness into our awareness."

– LAO TZU

5 BENEFITS OF BECOMING A CONSCIOUS LEADER

A good friend of mine quit his job. He worked for a company that used shame, blame, and guilt as their primary motivators. He was determined to remove himself from the toxic fumes of this daily culture. He was done living below the line.

Below the Line

Leaders who operate below the line breed cultures of drama, defensiveness, and scarcity. They tend to hold the belief that being right is the most important thing. They often argue, fight, find fault, and are quick to cast blame on others. These below the line leaders are unaware of their beliefs, behaviors, and the statements that often spew out of their mouths.

Becoming a Conscious Leader

Conscious leaders, who operate above the line, breed cultures of trust and acceptance. They tend to hold the belief that it's more valuable to learn and grow than it is to be right. They are present, curious, listen consciously, and take responsibility for their actions. Above the line leaders are aware of the beliefs, behaviors, and the statements that thoughtfully come out of their mouths.

One of the greatest ways to evolve as a conscious leader is to ask yourself daily, "Where Am I?" This question primes our conscious mind to turn inward and reflect on where we are relative to being *above* or *below* the line. A brief video from the Conscious Leadership Group demonstrates this brilliantly (Google: "Locating Yourself – A Key to Conscious Leadership").

Staying Above the Line

It's hard to stay above the line. Our primal brain actually prefers that we operate below the line. This is how we are hard-wired to operate – constantly ready to go into fight-or-flight mode, which our ancestors spent the bulk of their waking state in. The difference now is we don't have to hunt daily for our food or walk 30 miles to find water!

Instead, we need to find ways to slow down in order to turn inward and shift from the worry and fear that often come with being below the line. Shifting our awareness can empower us to live above the line and do things like:

1. Find time to meditate in our chaotic schedules.
2. Speak unarguably in a room full of stakeholders.
3. Appreciate all of the blessings our days are filled with.
4. Stay curious and willing to see things from another person's perspective.
5. Most importantly, above the line leaders take responsibility for their mental, physical, and spiritual health.

Staying Aware

It's not necessarily good or bad to be above or below the line. It's more about having the awareness to acknowledge how you are feeling and create space to shift when you are below the line. Conscious leaders make a daily commitment to be mindful of their location and share it with those around them. Always remember that the first step starts with knowing your location!

COURAGE TO CONNECT OFFLINE

Take a moment to assess how you are feeling in this current moment. Write down what you are feeling and where in your body you are feeling it.

Now, ask yourself if you are feeling above or below the line. Write down your response below.

COURAGE TO CONNECT ONLINE

Are there digital habits that you have developed that keep you below the line? Identify one below and jot down how you plan to be more aware of it.

"The purpose
of thinking
about the future
is not to predict
it but to raise
people's hopes."

— FREEMAN DYSON

The Digital Invasion

One of my favorite TED talks was by Adam Alter that discussed why our screen time makes us less happy. Over the past ten years, Alter demonstrates how our personal space (defined as the time spent beyond working, sleeping, and eating) has been invaded by our screens and social media as depicted in the orange area below. The yellow time indicates our endangered 'personal time.'

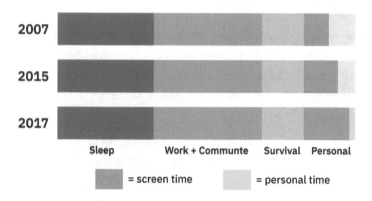

Our personal time is what defines our sense of self. Our hobbies, interests, and times of reflection are invaded by social media and smartphones. But this is old news and something I've talked about for the past decade. What I'm interested in now is turning the corner to begin sharing what the future of digital wellness looks like.

The Future of Digital Wellness

I'm confident that digital wellness is on the rise. In the past year alone Google, Apple, and Facebook have begun to establish their views on digital wellness and ways their future products and platforms will be more human-centered. Thought leaders throughout the world have begun discussing digital citizenship and the ethical arguments that will shape policy around the Internet and our device usage. So how does this ground-swell in digital wellness shape our future?

My Predictions

In addition to digital hippies, here are a few more predictions to make you ponder and maybe even laugh!

- The government is beginning to pilot communication policies within certain industries. These pilot policies include:

  - Sending a maximum of five emails a day per employee. Going over your quota can be considered 'email abuse,' a violation your organization can write you up for.

  - The workday ends at 4:00 p.m. and all devices stay at the office. This was influenced by a study from Harvard that showed healthy family structure is the number one indicator of economic development and low crime rates. People leave work and go home to their families, friends, and hobbies.

- Google has developed a smartphone that locks you out of it if you're too stressed. Fueled by astronomical levels of exhaustion and burnout, Google responded by creating a camera system that uses biometrics to measure stress and anxiety in the user. It's helped smartphone addicts curb their addiction by 50%.

- Facebook and Zoom have merged platforms as a response to the increase in remote workforce and purpose economy, demanding a more human-centered work-life experience.

- Tik-Tok has become the main platform for kids to learn how to dance and excersise.

Smoking, Seat Belts, and Recycling

Here are three reasons why my predictions may be heading in the right direction:

1. **Smoking** was at an all time high in the 1940's. It's been said that Generation Alpha (after Gen Z) will end smoking all together.

2. **Seat Belts** weren't required in cars until 1964. There had been 50 years

of driving since the Model-T was launched that didn't include seat belts!

3. **Reduce. Reuse. Recycle.** This was a campaign launched in the early 90's when I was in middle school. I had to train my parents on why recycling was vital to the future of our environment. Now it's second nature to recycle.

Your Digital Wellness

Do my predictions sound as foolish as a 20-hour work week? Maybe? Maybe not!

As we continue to press into the future of digital wellness, I encourage you to raise your awareness on how the content you view each day shapes your thought life and overall health.

Doing so can break through the ways in which content shapes our reality and allows us to look inward for our sense of purpose and worth. This my friends, is the most sacred part of being a warm-blooded creature, not a cold-blooded device. Here's to the future of Digital Wellness!

COURAGE TO CONNECT OFFLINE

Do you know any digital hippies in your life? Take some time and reach out to someone that appears to have their digital life in order. Ask them questions on the pros and cons of this lifestyle and see if you can glean any wisdom.

COURAGE TO CONNECT ONLINE

Start sharing ways that you want to embrace a healthy digital lifestyle. Use social media to share your ideas and even pose questions to your network to see if they too have ideas on how to improve their digital well-being.

CONCLUSION

You made it!

Thank you for reading the stories and resources within this book.

Conclusion

As you reflect on what you've learned, I have a few final hopes for you:

- I hope that you've gained clarity on how you were made to connect with the people in your life.

- I hope that you are feeling energized in ways that you can share your story and heart with those around you.

- I hope that you give yourself permission to spend more time restoring areas in your life that require your energy.

I encourage you to take your newfound courage beyond the words of this book. Your impact in life comes from offering the things you have to those around you. This impact happens even on days when you feel inadequate. All that you have to do is offer your time, resources, or even just lend an ear to listen to someone's situation. Finally, never underestimate the power you have in sharing your story or shaping someone else's. Always remember that you were made to connect with courage!

Acknowledgments

This book would not have been possible without the love and support of my wife. Ksenija, you've been so patient and encouraging. Thanks for all of your late-night editing, early morning conversations, and reminders not to overcomplicate things. I love and appreciate you so much.

Thank you to all of the people who shaped these stories. I've learned that people come in and out of your life for various reasons. I'm thankful for those that have walked through mine.

Thank you, God, for leading me in writing this book. I'm learning to draw my strength and confidence from You daily.

I'd like to say a special thanks to Loren Siffring, Mike Fencil, Sean Buono, and Michael Hahn. Your combined wisdom, prayers, and encouragement have laid a foundation for me to rest on.

Thank you to Joe 'JB' Klecha and Mike 'Mekal' Gentile for helping edit the stories along the way. A special thank you to Shawn McConnell for always taking time to read the stories and make them better. I also want to thank Sunshine, Alissa Klein, and Drew Patrick for the support in helping craft my messaging and brand.

A very special thank you to Laura Lybeer-Hilpert for designing this book and laying out the pages in a creative way. You are so great to work with!

A huge thanks to Stacey Turczyn for helping professinaly copyedit this book.

Thank you to my parents who taught me how to be empathic and share my heart with the world. Thank you to my siblings who understand me and still love me.

And thank YOU for reading this book and reflecting on ways that you can find the courage to connect in your online and offline life.

With Gratitude,

Other Available Resources

GRATITUDE NOTEBOOKS

Encourge a habit of gratitude within your family or company!

markostach.com/gratitude-notebook/

About the Author

Mark Ostach helps people find the courage to connect – with themselves, their purpose, and with the people in their lives, both online and offline. Mark's goal is to restore energy and focus to organizations battling modern-life's non-stop pace and growing sense of disconnection.

Mark knows what it's like to feel disconnected, having compulsively checked his phone for over a decade. He's on a mission to teach people healthy digital habits so they can improve their digital wellness and create deeper connections with things in life that matter most.

Mark holds degrees in psychology and technology with an interest in behavioral neuroscience. A nationally recognized speaker on Digital Wellness, Mark has done two TED talks and spoken to thousands of people all over the country encouraging them to embrace a culture of digital well-being.

In his free time, Mark likes to write music, spend time in nature, and enjoy life with his wife and their two children. He is determined to remind the world that human connection is the most powerful connection we have.

For speaking, coaching, and consulting inquires, please e-mail him at **hello@markostach.com.**